THE WAY
PEOPLE
LIVE

Life of a Roman Gladiator

THE WAY
PEOPLE
LIVE

Life of a Roman Gladiator

Titles in The Way People Live series include:

THE WAY PEOPLE LIVE

Life of a Roman Gladiator

by Don Nardo

LUCENT BOOKS®

THOMSON

GALE

San Diego • Detroit • New York • San Francisco • Cleveland • New Haven, Conn. • Waterville, Maine • London • Munich

LIBRARY OF CONGRESS CATALOGING-IN-PUBLICATION DATA

Nardo, Don, 1947–
    Life of a Roman gladiator / by Don Nardo.
        p. cm. — (The way people live)
Summary: Discusses aspects of the life of Roman gladiators, including recruitment,
training, weapons, and tactics, as well as how gladiatorial conflicts reflect the values
of their day.
Includes bibliographical references and index.
    ISBN 1-59018-253-7
    1. Gladiators—Juvenile literature. [1. Gladiators. 2. Rome—History—Republic,
265–30 B.C.] I. Title. II. Series.
    GV35.N35 2003
    796'.0937—dc21
                                                                    2002154014

Printed in the United States of America

Contents

Discovering the Humanity in Us All

Books in The Way People Live series focus on groups of people in a wide variety of circumstances, settings, and time periods. Some books focus on different cultural groups, others, on people in a particular historical time period, while others cover people involved in a specific event. Each book emphasizes the daily routines, personal and historical struggles, and achievements of people from all walks of life.

To really understand any culture, it is necessary to strip the mind of the common notions we hold about groups of people. These stereotypes are the archenemies of learning. It does not even matter whether the stereotypes are positive or negative; they are confining and tight. Removing them is a challenge that is not easily met, as anyone who has ever tried it will admit. Ideas that do not fit into the templates we create are unwelcome visitors—ones we would prefer remain quietly in a corner or forgotten room.

The cowboy of the Old West is a good example of such confining roles. The cowboy was courageous, yet soft-spoken. His time (it is always a he, in our template) was spent alternatively saving a rancher's daughter from certain death on a runaway stagecoach, or shooting it out with rustlers. At times, of course, he was likely to get a little crazy in town after a trail drive, but for the most part, he was the epitome of inner strength. It is disconcerting to find out that the cowboy is human, even a bit childish. Can it really be true that cowboys would line up to help the cook on the trail drive grind coffee, just hoping he would give them a little stick of peppermint candy that came with the coffee shipment? The idea of tough cowboys vying with one another to help "Coosie" (as they called their cooks) for a bit of candy seems silly and out of place.

So is the vision of Eskimos playing video games and watching MTV, living in prefab housing in the Arctic. It just does not fit with what "Eskimo" means. We are far more comfortable with snow igloos and whale blubber, harpoons and kayaks.

Although the cultures dealt with in Lucent's The Way People Live series are often historically and socially well known, the emphasis is on the personal aspects of life. Groups of people, while unquestionably affected by their politics and their governmental structures, are more than those institutions. How do people in a particular time and place educate their children? What do they eat? And how do they build their houses? What kinds of work do they do? What kinds of games do they enjoy? The answers to these questions bring these cultures to life. People's lives are revealed in the particulars and only by knowing the particulars can we understand these cultures' will to survive and their moments of weakness and greatness.

This is not to say that understanding politics does not help to understand a culture. There is no question that the Warsaw ghetto, for example, was a culture that was brought about by the politics and social ideas of Adolf

Hitler and the Third Reich. But the Jews who were crowded together in the ghetto cannot be understood by the Reich's politics. Their life was a day-to-day battle for existence, and the creativity and methods they used to prolong their lives is a vital story of human perseverance that would be denied by focusing only on the institutions of Hitler's Germany. Knowing that children as young as five or six outwitted Nazi guards on a daily basis, that Jewish policemen helped the Germans control the ghetto, that children attended secret schools in the ghetto and even earned diplomas—these are the things that reveal the fabric of life, that can inspire, intrigue, and amaze.

Books in The Way People Live series allow both the casual reader and the student to see humans as victims, heroes, and onlookers. And although humans act in ways that can fill us with feelings of sorrow and revulsion, it is important to remember that "hero," "predator," and "victim" are dangerous terms. Heaping undue pity or praise on people reduces them to objects, and strips them of their humanity.

Seeing the Jews of Warsaw only as victims is to deny their humanity. Seeing them only as they appear in surviving photos, staring at the camera with infinite sadness, is limiting, both to them and to those who want to understand them. To an object of pity, the only appropriate response becomes "Those poor creatures!" and that reduces both the quality of their struggle and the depth of their despair. No one is served by such two-dimensional views of people and their cultures.

With this in mind, The Way People Live series strives to flesh out the traditional, two-dimensional views of people in various cultures and historical circumstances. Using a wide variety of primary quotations—the words not only of the politicians and government leaders, but of the real people whose lives are being examined—each book in the series attempts to show an honest and complete picture of a culture removed from our own by time or space.

By examining cultures in this way, the reader will notice not only the glaring differences from his or her own culture, but also will be struck by the similarities. For indeed, people share common needs—warmth, good company, stability, and affirmation from others. Ultimately, seeing how people really live, or have lived, can only enrich our understanding of ourselves.

Gladiators: Artifacts of a Different Worldview

In the ancient world, which lacked daily newspapers, television, radio, the Internet, and other means of conveying news and advertising, people often painted ads on city walls. Archaeologists have found many such ads among the abundant graffiti on the walls of Pompeii, a Roman city buried and preserved by the eruption of the nearby volcano Mt. Vesuvius in A.D. 79. One news flash reads,

> Twenty pairs of gladiators sponsored by Decimus Lucretius Satrius Valens . . . and ten pairs of gladiators sponsored by Decimus Lucretius Valens, his son, will fight in Pompeii on April 8, 9, 10, 11, and 12. There will also be a suitable wild animal hunt.[1]

This was exciting news at the time. Gladiatorial combats were not everyday events, in large part because they were very expensive to stage. So, people reading this ad no doubt looked forward to the scheduled bouts, much as people today happily anticipate the upcoming day of a major sporting event or concert.

The ad is instructive, not only in what it told those who read it but also in what it did not bother to tell them. It provides the names of the citizens who paid for the event, for example. But it does not mention that these sponsors usually owned the fighters they presented and that the combatants had no choice but to fight when and where they were told to. This was common knowledge at the time, just as everyone today knows, without being reminded, that a rock concert will feature drums and guitars.

Similarly, the ad did not need to tell people that the upcoming combats would be bloody and that there was a good chance that several of the sixty fighters involved would be killed. (Not all matches ended in death. Another piece of Pompeiian graffiti mentions an exhibition of nine matches during which only three men were killed; the other six losers were spared, presumably for performing with unusual skill or bravery.) Indeed, not only was everyone aware of the chance of death in the arena, it was actually a major factor in the mass appeal of such public games. Put simply, most Romans loved spectacle sports, especially violent ones, and usually the more violent, the better. These violent sports included single combats between men and men (and sometimes women); staged battles involving larger groups of combatants, each group representing an enemy army or navy; and combats between men and beasts. For at least four centuries, Romans of all walks of life flocked to amphitheaters (the oval-shaped structures where such games were held) and cheered as they watched both humans and animals face danger and often gruesome death.

Ancient Versus Modern Standards

It is important to stress that not all Romans were thrilled with violent arena combats. A small minority of intellectuals found these spectacles needlessly cruel, pointless, or low class, or held that they corroded one's ethics and encouraged bad behavior. "Nothing is so injurious to [one's] character as lounging at the [public] shows," remarked the first-century-A.D. playwright and philosopher Seneca the Younger. "Pleasure [at seeing others suffer] paves an easy way for vice to creep in [to your own life]."[2] Roman Christians went even further, condemning the killing in gladiatorial combats as murder. In about A.D. 200, the Christian theologian Tertullian wrote,

> He who shudders at the body of a man who died by nature's law, the common death of all, will, in the amphitheater, gaze down with most tolerant eyes on the bodies of

men mangled, torn to pieces, defiled with their own blood; yes, and he who comes to the spectacle [in effect signifies] his approval of murder.[3]

Needless to say, most observers in modern times have agreed with Tertullian. And numerous writers, including a number of historians, have drawn the conclusion that the Romans must have been a cruel, mean-spirited, or bloodthirsty people at heart. How else can their enthusiasm for public maiming and killing be explained?

Such reasoning, however, is faulty. For one thing, the intellectuals and Christians (both educated and uneducated) who disliked arena fights were Romans, too. If all Romans, as a

One of the many modern cinematic scenes featuring Roman gladiators, from Italian director Enrico Guazzoni's 1922 film, Messalina.

people, were inherently savage and cruel, there would have been no such vocal minority criticizing the public games. The criticism from some Romans suggests that the love of gladiatorial fights and other violent shows was cultural and learned, not inborn. Also, a fascination with performances involving danger and the potential of injury and death is not limited to the ancient Romans. "Even today," classical scholar Eckart Kohne points out,

> spectators relish pictures of catastrophes, or sports in which accidents or even the death of the participants may be expected. . . . Modern television transmissions of fatal crashes in motor racing spring to mind; the media bring them into our houses, and the danger to which the drivers in their powerful cars are exposed plays a considerable part in our enjoyment. . . . Other sports, such as [boxing and ultimate fighting], also benefit in the public mind from the similar risks they entail. Naturally the gladiatorial contests of the ancient world are in no way comparable with the sports mentioned above. These contests sanctioned mortal combat between one man and another, and made the death of the loser the general rule, displaying a total lack of moral and ethical principles that are generally accepted in modern times. But the value system of Roman society differed from our own in this point, and we cannot apply today's standards in making moral judgments.[4]

Kohne's last point, that it is inappropriate to judge an ancient society by modern standards, is critical in giving the Romans their due as great and key players on history's stage. As English scholar Alan Baker puts it,

> To apply our own values to a civilization two thousand years removed in history is

absurd, and will certainly not help us to understand the [gladiatorial] games or the reasons for their development. In our own age, human life is prized and respected above all else (at least in theory); to inflict suffering on others for the sake of enjoyment is considered perverse and incomprehensible. But such a perspective simply did not exist in the ancient world.[5]

Death as an Honor and Duty

The Roman perspective on death in the arena was part of a different value system than the one widely accepted today. In a world where conquest of neighboring lands was an accepted fact of life everywhere, the Romans were experts at subjugating and ruling others. Those who did not share or learn to embrace Roman culture were seen as barbarians or at least as inferior; either way, the Romans believed that using force against them was fully warranted. At the same time, military culture—consisting of the life, deeds, tribulations, and values of the soldiers who made Rome's conquests possible—was highly venerated, and to die fighting for the fatherland was viewed as a great service and honor.

Not surprisingly, such martial values filtered down into other aspects of Roman society, including entertainment. Gladiators were often criminals or foreigners captured in wars; moreover, the outfits these fighters wore were modeled after those of foreign warriors. This allowed little pity for the combatants in the arena, who represented (sometimes literally, other times symbolically) dangerous forces threatening the Roman state. Also, if a gladiator wanted to prove he was a true man and soldier, he showed his

Many modern sports fans enjoy dangerous and bloody combat sports such as boxing and ultimate fighting. The winner of this 1996 ultimate fighting bout won $50,000 for beating his opponent senseless.

courage and devotion to duty by fighting and, if necessary, dying for his "betters" (in this case, the Roman spectators). In the words of Stephen Wisdom, author of a popular recent book on gladiators,

> Such [gladiatorial] displays reinforced the superiority of Rome over the barbarian enemy, and provided an entertaining and spectacular day out for the Roman mob.

. . . The Romans believed that gladiatorial spectacles allowed the condemned combatants to display a quality rooted in Roman moral values, that of *virtus*, or virtue. They had the chance to show bravery and spirit as they were attacked; in death they elevated their barbarian lives to a higher level. They may not have embraced Roman culture, but they could at least die like Romans should.[6]

Therefore, Roman gladiators and all the violence and blood associated with them must not be viewed through the prism of modern sensibilities and ethical rules. Rather, these fighters are better seen as artifacts of a different worldview and value system. That system is now outmoded. Yet the idea of gladiatorial bouts still inspires fascination and excitement in modern audiences, as evidenced by the success of movies such as *Spartacus* and *Gladiator* and the establishment of numerous gladiator reenactor groups. The blood spilled in the fights staged for these venues is not real, of course. But the nostalgia and admiration for a long-dead sport, however bloody and cruel, is real enough.

The Origins of Roman Gladiators

The exact origins of the famous gladiatorial combats in which men and women fought to the death to entertain crowds of spectators are still uncertain and often disputed by scholars. For a long time, the accepted theory was that the Romans adopted these combats, called *munera* (singular, *munus*), from the Etruscans. The Etruscans were a robust, culturally advanced people who inhabited the region directly north of Rome (then known as Etruria, today as Tuscany). The Etruscan city-states exerted a strong cultural influence over the early Romans, who freely borrowed numerous artistic and social concepts from their more refined neighbors.

According to this view, the Romans were particularly impressed by Etruscan funeral rites, which operated under the belief that, when an important man died, his spirit required a blood sacrifice to survive in the afterlife. Supposedly, the spirits of the dead would not be satisfied until they received an infusion of fresh blood from someone still living. (In fact, the literal translation of *munera* is "duties" or "offerings" to the dead.) It was the duty of the dead person's relatives to carry out this sacrifice. Thus, in very ancient times, it was customary for the family and friends of a deceased warrior to sacrifice one or more war prisoners on or near his tomb. Likely, their throats were cut and the blood allowed to sink into the ground; this would nourish and appease not only the man's spirit but also those of his dead relatives.

In time, the practice of literal human sacrifice gave way to rituals in which the men sacrificed were not killed outright but given the chance to fight for their lives. According to the second-century-A.D. Roman scholar Festus, "It was the custom to sacrifice prisoners on the tombs of valorous [courageous] warriors; when the cruelty of this custom became evident, it was decided to make gladiators fight before the tomb."[7] Thus, these fights, which were still rather simple and witnessed by the mourners rather than the public, became part of the funeral rituals of some well-to-do Etruscan and later Roman families.

The Greek Connection

This scenario may well be substantially accurate, except for the insistence that the Romans got the idea from the Etruscans. The fact is that the Etruscans, as well as a number of other early Italian peoples, including the Romans themselves, were strongly influenced by the Greeks. In the late 700s and early 600s B.C., Greek settlers began establishing cities in southern Italy, and these cities quickly became prosperous and highly influential in the region.

Along with other aspects of their rich culture, the newcomers brought with them their legends of the Trojan War, as told by the legendary Greek poet Homer in his great epic the *Iliad*. This tale contains, among other things, a striking example of the early Greek funeral rituals performed for great warriors

This drawing, based on a Greek vase painting now displayed in the Louvre, in Paris, shows an episode of funeral combat from Homer's Iliad.

slain in battle. When the hero Patroclus is killed by a Trojan prince, Achilles, one of the leaders of the Greek expedition against Troy (and the central character of the *Iliad*), sacrifices twelve Trojan youths at Patroclus's tomb. "Fare thee well Patroclus," Achilles says, "even in the grave fare thee well. See, I now fulfill all that I promised you before. Here are the twelve noble sons of Trojans—the fire is eating them round about you!"[8] The Greeks then hold athletic games in Patroclus's honor. In one of these contests, two Greek champions—Ajax and Diomedes—engage in single combat with swords and shields, also in honor of the slain Patroclus. Thus, the *Iliad* describes both of the funerary customs mentioned by Festus—human sacrifice and gladiatorial-style combat.

The Romans were duly impressed by Greek culture, including the characters and ideas of the *Iliad*. And there is ample evidence of their borrowing some of these characters and ideas. For example, perhaps because they had no ancestral heroes of their own who quite compared in stature with those who fought at Troy, the Romans attempted to create a link between themselves and one of the leading characters of the Trojan story. It appears that at least by the sixth century B.C. Roman legends had incorporated the tale of the Trojan prince Aeneas's escape from the burning Troy. Eventually, according to Roman myth, Aeneas made a fateful journey to Italy and there established the Roman race.

It is not necessary, therefore, to invoke the Etruscans as middlemen who funneled early Greek funerary customs to the Romans. The Romans likely adopted these ideas themselves, directly from the Greeks. Indeed, Festus does not specifically mention the Etruscans when describing the custom of human sacrifice at the tombs of prominent men, and there is no reason to think he was not talking about a Roman custom.

Origins in Campania?

A number of scholars argue that the transition from straightforward human sacrifice to staged fights between warriors at the funerals of Roman noblemen first occurred in Campania. Campania was the fertile region surrounding the Gulf of Cumae (now the Bay of Naples) on Italy's southwestern coast. (Mt. Vesuvius and Pompeii were major landmarks in Campania.) The modern discovery of paintings in Campania dating to the mid–fourth century B.C. has shed some important light on the birth of the gladi-atorial concept. The paintings, which are quite detailed and splendid in execution, emerged in southern Italy, most of the best in Paestum, a town in the Campania region. These works show a variety of events that took place at funeral games, including chariot racing, boxing, and fights between pairs of heavily armed warriors. A particularly revealing point, according to Eckart Kohne, is that

in some cases a referee is shown standing beside these pairs of men, [so] they can only have been involved in contests in

A nineteenth-century engraving shows pairs of warriors fighting at an early Roman funeral. This custom eventually gave rise to formal gladiatorial combats.

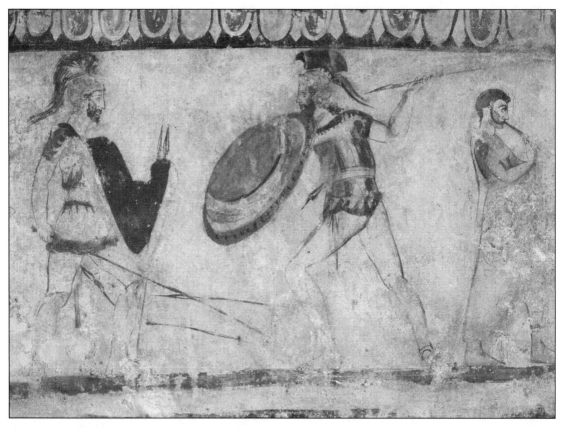

Among the wall paintings discovered at Paestum, in Campania, is this one showing warriors fighting as part of a funeral ritual. Gladiatorial bouts probably originated in Campania.

honor of the dead [since the presence of a referee indicates that the combat was staged rather than part of standard warfare], a direct parallel to the later *munera* in Rome. It is doubtful whether the term "gladiator" can be used at this early period, for nothing is known of the origin and position in life of any of the men depicted. Nonetheless, there are other arguments in favor of identifying Campania as the area where gladiator fights originated. The first stone amphitheaters were built there [the very first at Pompeii], and it was the site of the most important gladiator schools [including the one at Capua, from which the famous gladiator Spartacus escaped].[9]

The great first-century-B.C. Roman historian Livy also connects Campania with early gladiatorial combats, in this case involving the Samnites. In fact, this incident appears to be the origin of the standard and popular gladiator type known as the "Samnite." The Samnites were a sturdy, often warlike people who inhabited the valleys of Italy's central and southern Apennine Mountains. In the middle of the fourth century B.C., Samnite territory and population were probably twice as big as those of Rome and the largest of any single Italian people. The Romans

The First Stone Amphitheaters

The town of Pompeii, in Campania, where gladiators had originated, erected Italy's first all-stone amphitheater in about the year 80 B.C. Less than two centuries later (A.D. 79), the great eruption of nearby Mt. Vesuvius encased the town in a protective layer of ash, so the amphitheater is extremely well preserved. In fact, the inscription carved to dedicate the building still survives. The names of the two public officials who oversaw the project—Valgus and Porcius—are plainly visible. Because the Latin term *amphitheatrum* had not yet been coined, the inscription refers to the structure as a *spectaculum*, or a "place for spectacles."

Visitors today also marvel at the size and dimensions of the Pompeiian amphitheater. Its oval bowl measures 445 by 341 feet and originally sat about twenty thousand people, nearly the entire population of the town. The arena floor, where the gladiators and animals grappled and died, is recessed below the level of the outside ground. That ground forms a huge earthen embankment that backs into and helps support the great weight of many of the rising tiers of stone seats. An outer perimeter of high brick arches and several large exterior staircases provide added support for the structure's curved walls.

Although they remain in an excellent state of preservation, the amphitheater's ruins give only the barest hint of what the building was like in its heyday. Numerous comforts and amenities that the crowds of spectators enjoyed are no longer visible. Among these amenities were elegant decorations such as statues and tapestries; cushions to sit on; fast-food stands surrounding the complex and vendors selling refreshments in the stands; and a huge awning (*velarium*) that shaded the audience on hot sunny days.

Visible beyond the edge of the smaller of Pompeii's two theaters (in foreground) is the city's gladiatorial barracks and training ground.

fought three wars against the Samnites; in the second (326–304 B.C.), the Samnites invaded Campania and occupied the town of Neapolis (Naples). Eventually, the Romans defeated the intruders, after which the victors held a large triumph (parade) to show off the prisoners and weapons they had captured. According to Livy,

> By far the greatest sight in the procession was the captured armor, and so magnificent were the pieces considered that the gilded shields were distributed amongst the owners of the silversmiths' shops to adorn the Forum [Rome's main town square]. . . . While the Romans made use of this armor to honor the gods, the Campanians, out of contempt and hatred towards the Samnites, made the gladiators who performed at their banquets wear it, and they then called them "Samnites." [10]

The First Gladiators in Rome

As time went on, gladiatorial combats, still staged only occasionally at the funerals of prominent individuals, caught on beyond Campania. The first known contest between gladiators in the city of Rome took place in 264 B.C. Two young aristocrats, Marcus and Decimus Brutus Pera, honored the memory of their father, Junius, by arranging for three pairs of warriors to fight at the funeral games. The combats were held in the Forum Boarium, a commercial market located between the Palatine hill and Tiber River. The term *gladiator* had apparently still not been coined; the fighters, who were slaves, were called *bustuarii*, probably meaning "tomb men" or "tomb fighters." By this time also, the ceremonial combat itself was referred to as a *munus*, or duty to the dead, the name it would bear for centuries to come.

In the years following this event, the custom of staging *munera* at funerals evidently grew in popularity in the Roman capital. The fights also increased in scope. Later literary references to such combats by Roman writers mention increasingly large numbers of fighters. For example, Livy says that in 215 B.C., at the height of the bloody Second Punic War (against Carthage),

> In honor of Marcus Aemilius Lepidus, who had been augur and twice consul [one of Rome's two jointly serving administrator generals], his three sons, Lucius, Marcus, and Quintus, organized funeral games lasting three days, including the exhibition in the Forum of twenty-two pairs of gladiators. [11]

Fifteen years later, another Roman notable—Marcus Valerius Laevinus—was memorialized by twenty-five pairs of gladiators; seventeen years after that (183 B.C.), sixty pairs fought at the funeral of Publius Licinius; and in 174 B.C., thirty-four pairs of gladiators clashed over the tomb of the dead military hero Titus Quinctius Flamininus. (Though fewer fighters commemorated Flamininus's passing than Licinius's, the funeral given Flamininus by his son lasted four days and included a huge public banquet, the distribution of large amounts of food to the populace, and the presentation of plays.)

These and the other early *munera* staged in Rome were still infrequent events, partly because only a few wealthy individuals could afford to buy or hire (through a slave owner), as well as arm and train, so many fighters. They were also still largely private affairs that either were closed to the general public or admitted a limited number of public spectators, depending on how much room was available in the area where the combats took place.

The scene in this old engraving is an artist's depiction of fighters taking part in funeral games held during the early years of the Republic.

As for the area itself, before the first permanent stone amphitheaters were built in the first century B.C. and first century A.D., gladiators fought in wide, open areas, most often the fora (plural of forum) or the marketplaces of cities. A major piece of evidence for this fact is a reference made by the first-century-B.C. Roman architect and engineer Vitruvius in his *De architectura* ("On Architecture"): "The custom of giving gladiatorial shows in the Forum has been handed down from our ancestors."[12]

As demand for gladiatorial shows increased, spectators likely began to complain about having to stand for long periods of time; also, only those in the front rows had clear, unobstructed views of the action. So the sponsors of the games eventually began providing seats. At first, these probably consisted of consecutive rows of wooden benches erected in or around the fora or marketplaces where the fights were staged. However, in time these makeshift wooden facilities became separate, freestanding buildings in their own right. Some

This fanciful sixteenth-century oil painting purports to show gladiators fighting in Rome's main Forum, as described by the ancient writer Vitruvius.

were dismantled and reassembled as need dictated. Others may have stood intact for several seasons before being demolished to make way for houses, temples, or other structures. Alan Baker offers this general description of the spectators and fighters in this formative era of the *munera:*

> They were watched by very few spectators, who had to squeeze in against each other, pushing and jostling, straining and craning their necks to get a look at the bloody action being played out before them. These rough congregations, in which the spectators quickly planted themselves wherever they could find a place with a decent view, contained the

seeds of the great spectacles of later years. . . . At this stage, the *munera* were still viewed exclusively in terms of religious ceremony, this feeling perhaps enhanced by the very close quarters at which the battles were experienced. Women were not allowed to attend. It was not long, however, before seats were added and hired out to the spectators, who were thus afforded a little more comfort as they watched each pair of gladiators fight. At this stage, they were all armed in the same manner: that of the Samnites. . . . Each gladiator would carry a long, rectangular shield (*scutum*), a straight sword (*gladius*, from which the word "gladiator" derives), a helmet, and greaves (leg armor).[13]

From Religious Ritual to Entertainment

Even if the number of spectators at such combats was small at first, those who did manage to get seats were enthralled, and these fights to the death became eagerly awaited events. As public demand for attendance to the combats grew, the simple, small-scale, and largely informal *munera* meant to honor dead warriors gave way to public displays increasingly viewed as entertainment. In fact, in the second and first centuries B.C. (the last years of the Roman Republic), gladiatorial fights, along with other violent kinds of public shows, emerged as Rome's most popular form of entertainment. (In addition to contests between gladiators, these included wild beast hunts, which appeared on the same program with the *munera*, and the "combat sport" of boxing, the Roman version of which was extremely dangerous and bloody.)

All other kinds of entertainment, including plays staged in theaters, had much smaller followings and increasingly found themselves unable to compete with the more violent attractions. Evidence for the growing craze for gladiators comes from the surviving works of the Roman playwright Terence (Publius Terentius Afer, ca. 185–ca. 159 B.C.). To Terence's dismay, both his first and second attempts to stage his play *The Mother-in-Law* (in 165 B.C. and five years later) failed when the audiences either rushed away or demanded to see what they viewed as more exciting shows. In the surviving prologue of the play, written for the third attempt to produce it (which succeeded), Terence recalls,

At the first production, much talk of some boxers . . . forced me off the stage before the end. I then decided to . . . put it on a second time. The first part was doing well when news arrived that there was to be a gladiatorial show [in the theater]. In surged the people, pushing, shouting, jostling for a place, leaving me powerless to hold my own.[14]

From then on, public demand for bigger and more exciting gladiatorial shows grew faster than ever. In 65 B.C., the renowned military general Julius Caesar became the first Roman leader to stage really large-scale *munera* as entertainment, a shrewd move designed to increase his popularity and prestige with the Roman masses. He was so confident in the drawing power of gladiators that he did not hesitate to pay for the show out of his own pocket (which he could well afford). Caesar's first-century-B.C. Greek biographer, Plutarch

Julius Caesar, the famed military general, presented a large-scale gladiatorial show in 65 B.C.

of Chaeronea, reported that Caesar presented 320 pairs of gladiators. [15] And Plutarch's contemporary, the Roman historian Suetonius (Gaius Suetonius Tranquillus, ca. A.D. 69–ca. 140), gave these fascinating details:

> Caesar put on a gladiatorial show, but had collected so immense a troop of combatants that his terrified political opponents [fearing that the gladiators might rebel, as had occurred in the uprising led by the gladiator Spartacus a few years before, or that Caesar might use these warriors to stage a government coup] rushed a bill through the [legislature], limiting the number of gladiators that anyone might keep in Rome; consequently far fewer pairs fought than had been advertised. [16]

Caesar was also largely responsible for the transition from the older system of training, managing, and paying for gladiators to the one that became standard in the two centuries following his death. Before his time, all *munera* were privately funded, and a well-to-do person who desired to stage a gladiatorial show went to a *lanista*, a professional supplier who found and trained the fighters. Caesar wanted to give the state more control over these fights, so he erected a gladiator school (*ludus*) run by senators and other prestigious Romans. The first state-funded public *munera* were held in 44 B.C., just before Caesar's assassination. And two years later the Roman aediles (officials in charge of maintaining public buildings and overseeing public games) created a sensation when they substituted gladiatorial bouts for chariot races on a public program. This opened the floodgates, so to speak, and thereafter the Roman people were completely hooked on gladiators. The first emperor, Augustus (formerly Octavian, Caesar's adopted son), recognized the potential for exploiting this public addiction for the state's advantage. He and his immediate successors made control and promotion of the *munera* virtually an imperial monopoly.

"Bread and Circuses"

However, this transition from small-scale, privately run *munera* to large-scale, state-sponsored versions was not a completely smooth one. During the last two centuries of the Republic, certain fears about staging major gladiatorial combats, as well as other public games that drew massive crowds, persisted, especially among men of wealth and power. Many feared that holding large-scale games in the capital city might pose a threat to public order. As had happened at Julius Caesar's *munus* in 65 B.C., some people worried that an unscrupulous politician might use his gladiators as a small but formidable army to take over the government.

Many senators and other government leaders also worried about what might happen when crowds of commoners attended *munera* and other large-scale games. There was a paranoid fear that the mob could become inflamed by the violence and blood they witnessed or perhaps use the opportunity of a large public assembly to protest against the authorities. Either way, the result might be civil disturbances or even open rebellion. For these reasons, the Senate, the most powerful government body during the Republic, long refused to approve the construction of large, permanent theaters and amphitheaters.

However, as the *munera* and other public games became increasingly popular, these fears proved groundless. In fact, the authorities learned that gladiatorial bouts, wild animal hunts, and other spectacles, when sponsored and controlled by the government, could actually be effective tools for keeping public order.

Julius Caesar and others showed that staging such events could garner public support as well. Presenting large-scale spectacles helped politicians win votes in late republican times. And in the early imperial years, when elections no longer determined leadership (because the emperors controlled the government), the emperors used the shows to foster or increase their personal popularity.

In this way, the *munera*, which had once consisted of small-scale private funerary rituals, became part of a deliberate twofold governmental policy. The state sponsored regular large-scale distributions of bread and other foodstuffs to the poor. By the late first century A.D., as many as 150,000 urban Romans received such handouts at hundreds of distribution centers located across the capital city. Senators, military generals, and emperors also came to spend huge sums subsidizing public festivals, shows, and games, including gladiato-

rial fights. This policy of appeasing the masses through both free food and entertainment eventually became known as *panem et circenses,* or "bread and circuses." (A circus was a long race-track used for chariot races, but the term was also used in a more generic sense to mean public games in general.) The Roman satirist Juvenal (Decimus Junius Juvenalis, ca. A.D. 60–ca. 130) is usually credited with coining the term. "There's only two things that concern" the commoners, he said, "bread and [circus] games."[17] The second-century-A.D. orator Marcus Cornelius Fronto provided a more detailed description of the bread and circuses policy. "Because of his shrewd understanding of political science," Fronto wrote,

the emperor [Trajan, who reigned from 98 to 117] gave his attention even to actors and other performers on stage or on the race track or in the arena, since he

The First Emperor Sponsors *Munera*

Augustus, the first emperor, wisely spent large sums staging gladiatorial bouts and the wild animal shows (*venationes*) that regularly accompanied them in the amphitheaters. He also presented large-scale fights between the crews of ships in mock naval battles (*naumachiae*). Augustus bragged about these accomplishments in the *Res gestae,* a summary of his achievements he compiled in his later life (quoted in Lewis and Reinhold's *Roman Civilization: Sourcebook II*).

"I gave a gladiatorial show three times in my own name, and five times in the names of my sons and grandsons; at these shows about 10,000 [gladiators] fought. . . . In my thirteenth consulship, I was the first to celebrate the Games of Mars, which . . . have

[been] regularly celebrated in the succeeding years. Twenty-six times I provided for the people, in my own name or in the names of my sons or grandsons, hunting spectacles of African wild beasts in the . . . amphitheaters; in these exhibitions about 3,500 animals were killed. I presented to the people an exhibition of a naval battle across the Tiber where the grove of the Caesars now is, having had the site excavated 1,800 feet in length and 1,200 feet in width. In this exhibition thirty beaked ships [ships equipped with rams on their bows], triremes [with three banks of oars] or biremes [with two banks], and in addition a great number of smaller vessels engaged in combat. On board these fleets, exclusive of rowers, there were about 3,000 combatants."

knew that the Roman people are held in control principally by two things—free grain and shows—that political support depends as much on the entertainments as on matters of serious import, that neglect of serious problems does the greater harm, but neglect of entertainments brings damaging unpopularity, that gifts [from the emperor] are less eagerly and ardently longed for than shows, and finally, that gifts placate [appease] only the common people on the grain dole, singly and individually, but the shows placate everyone.[18]

In addition, gladiatorial games helped the government maintain control of the masses

The gladiatorial bouts were eventually accompanied by wild beast shows. (This scene is completely fanciful. Usually only a few animals and hunters appeared in the arena at the same time.)

by acting as a sort of safety valve for the people's hostility or dissent. A custom evolved in which ordinary people with legitimate grievances approached the emperor or other high official at the amphitheater during a *munus* (or at the circus during the races). Those leaders who listened respectfully and offered at least some minimal favorable response found it helped them to maintain their popularity, at least for the moment. Noted scholar Alan Cameron elaborates:

> Provided that it did not get out of hand (and in the early Empire there were normally police provisions adequate to ensure that it did not), even a hostile demonstration could ease a difficult situation. A grievance aired, even if fruitlessly, is a grievance halved. Imagine the tension the first time Nero entered the theater after the murder of [his mother] Agrippina. A joke against him . . . if tolerated, could help to diffuse indignation that, if suppressed, might have smoldered and grown to explode in a much more dangerous way. . . . The games themselves could serve as a safety valve. Genuine grievances (about a tax, a corn shortage, a minister) would tend to be dissipated in the excitement [of the spectacle]. . . . There can be little doubt that, not least among their functions, the games did indeed divert popular attention

Painted Portraits of Gladiators

Paintings, including portraits, of popular gladiators became common in both private homes and public places during the late Republic (and into imperial times). The noted first-century-A.D. Roman scholar and encyclopedist Pliny the Elder commented on this brand of artwork in this excerpt from Book 35 of his huge *Natural History*.

"When a freedman of [the emperor] Nero was putting on a gladiatorial show at Antium, paintings containing life-like portraits of all the gladiators and their assistants decorated the public porticoes [roofed walkways]. Portraits of gladiators have commanded the greatest interest in art for many generations. It was, however, Gaius Terentius Lucanus who began commissioning pictures of gladiatorial shows and having them publicly exhibited."

from what, for most, were the grim and tedious realities of everyday life in Rome. [19]

In the span of three or four centuries, therefore, minor single combats originally intended to appease the dead evolved into major spectacles that appeased the living masses.

Recruitment, Training, and Discipline

Through skill, stamina, courage, and luck, a few gladiators managed to earn fame, fortune, and freedom. However, life for the vast majority of gladiators was anything but glamorous or rewarding. Most of those in the profession were seen by society as lowly, disreputable characters; only a few entered the gladiatorial ranks by choice; they had to surrender themselves and their destinies completely to people widely considered their "betters"; their training was physically hard and relentless; their quarters in the barracks of gladiator schools were spare and devoid of luxury; and they faced the very real prospect of permanent injury or death at an early age. Moreover, though many dreamed of rebelling against and escaping from this unpleasant life, few actually tried, and even fewer succeeded. The true essence of an ordinary gladiator's life did not consist of the relatively few moments he spent in the arena but of the long, grueling weeks, months, and sometimes years he spent preparing for those fateful moments.

How Gladiators Were Recruited

Most gladiators started out as slaves, criminals, or war captives, all of whom were unfree and forced into the profession (although the more successful ones could and often did eventually earn or buy their freedom). A minority of gladiatorial recruits were free individuals who volunteered to enter the gladiator schools. The percentage of volunteers in the ranks is uncertain; it was likely at least 10 percent and may have been considerably higher at times. Some individuals volunteered because they had financial difficulties; there was a sign-up bonus for volunteer gladiators and usually prize money for those who won in the arena. Other volunteers were perhaps motivated by the physical challenge and appeal of danger, or they thought they had a chance of becoming popular idols and sex symbols who could have their pick of pretty young girls (or boys). The many slogans painted onto Pompeii's walls include these two provocative ones: "Caladus, the Thracian, makes all the girls sigh," and "Crescens, the net fighter, holds the hearts of all the girls."[20] Whatever their reasons for volunteering, as noted scholar Michael Grant points out, these individuals "were generally derived from the lowest-ranking category of free persons, namely the freedmen who had themselves been slaves or were the sons of slaves."[21] Only rarely did members of the upper classes enter the gladiatorial ranks, and those who did so provoked scandal and ridicule.

As for the slaves and other unfree recruits, until the mid–first century B.C. the task of finding them fell on the *lanista*. This businessman and wholesaler of human merchandise scoured the countryside, islands, and markets far and wide looking for slaves or prisoners he could buy inexpensively. Undoubtedly, many *lanistae* were not above trading with some of the pirates who raided foreign coasts and kidnapped whole families or villages. Once he had collected a stable of fighters—his *familia gladiatorum,* or "family of gladiators"—a *lanista* could make a considerable profit from renting them out or occasionally selling them. His biggest customers were prominent republican officials (for instance, Julius Caesar when he was aedile in 65 B.C.), men who staged large *munera* and could afford to spend large sums to bolster their own public images.

However successful he might be financially, the *lanista* had to deal with a serious downside to his profession. Namely, his social status was little or no better than that of the persons he bought and sold; most Romans, including those who paid for his services, looked on a *lanista* as a vile and disreputable pimp. Thus, Roman society engaged in rather naked hypocrisy for the sake of people's convenience and self-indulgence. As Alan Baker puts it,

> While the *lanistae* may have been the objects of hatred and contempt in Roman society,

This painting captures the popularity of male gladiators with young women. The fighter standing at center has just killed his opponent in a match held at a private banquet.

they still made possible one of that society's favorite pastimes. So their moral objections did not stop the citizenry from enjoying the bloody spectacle of the gladiatorial combat on a regular basis.[22]

Furthermore, this hypocrisy was carried to another level in the case of upper-class individuals. A curious double standard existed between the *lanistae* who procured gladiators and those well-to-do men (and occasionally women) who bought and kept them in their own stables. While the *lanista* was scorned for his role in the process, the reputation of an upper-class Roman who maintained a gladiatorial troupe only as a sideline or extra source of income remained unblemished.

The *lanistae* were eventually forced to the sidelines, however. After Caesar's time, as the amphitheater games became larger in scope, the demand for new gladiatorial recruits tremendously increased. And the Roman state met that demand by monopolizing the procurement, maintenance, and training of gladiators. When the Romans won a battle against a foreign people, for instance, they selected an unspecified number of the prisoners—usually the healthiest and strongest—to become arena fighters. The state also obtained a few recruits of slave status by buying them from *lanistae*. *Lanistae* were now required to supply the *editor*, the man in charge of organizing the games, with a certain number of recruits at a low price.

Among the other sources of gladiatorial recruits were slave markets and private owners who made extra money by selling or hiring out their slaves for the arena. (For a long time, slaves had no choice but to obey their masters and become gladiators. In the second century, however, the enlightened emperor Hadrian modified the law, requiring a master either to get a slave's consent to become a gladiator or to show proof that the slave had committed a crime serious enough to warrant condemnation to the arena.) Still another source of new gladiators was a criminal penalty known as the *damnatio ad ludum*, meaning "condemned to the gladiator barracks." Some of the free indi-

This shot from the film Spartacus *shows some upper-class Romans reacting with fear and disgust as a gladiator loses his composure and threatens them.*

One of the few ancient written references to the gladiator's oath is found in the following excerpt from the thirty-seventh epistle (letter) in the *Moral Letters* of the first-century Roman philosopher Seneca. The theme of the text is how a person might consciously attain goodness. And Seneca makes the point that, unlike a gladiator, who unwillingly takes his oath to fight and die, a free man who desires to be virtuous must willingly swear to do so and then fight to maintain that state of goodness all his days, which is no easy task.

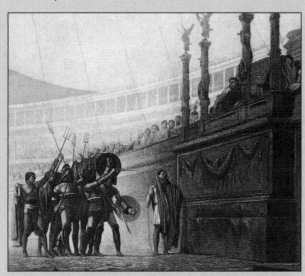

"You have promised to be a good man; you have enlisted under oath; that is the strongest chain which will hold you to a strongest understanding. Any man will be but mocking you, if he declares that this is an effeminate and easy kind of soldiering. I will not have you deceived. The words of this most honorable compact are the same as the words of that most disgraceful one, to wit: 'through burning, imprisonment, or death by the sword.' From the men who hire out their strength for the arena, who eat and drink what they must pay for with their blood, security is taken that they will endure such trials even though they be unwilling; from you, that you will endure them willingly and with alacrity. The gladiator may lower his weapon and test the pity of the people; but you will neither lower your weapon nor beg for life. You must die erect and unyielding. Moreover, what profit is it to gain a few days or a few years? There is no discharge for us from the moment we are born."

Gladiators salute the emperor before beginning their matches. Earlier, they swore to die by the sword.

viduals who were convicted of serious crimes (such as arson, military mutiny, murder, or treason) received this penalty rather than sentences of death or hard labor in the mines.

The Gladiator's Oath

Because of the government's growing monopoly on the *munera,* by the early first century A.D. the imperial *ludi* (short for *ludi gladiatoria,* meaning "gladiator schools" or "barracks") were the only authorized training facilities for arena fighters. Each school in Rome or other Italian cities was overseen by an official known as a *procurator;* in Rome's provinces, a *procurator* had charge of all the schools in his province.

The city of Rome had three imperial *ludi gladiatoria:* the *Ludus Gallicus, Ludus Dacicus,* and *Ludus Magnus.* (A fourth school—the

Surviving Remains of a Gladiator School

In this excerpt from his informative book on Roman gladiators, noted scholar Michael Grant describes the ruins of the gladiator school at Pompeii, which was preserved by the ash from the A.D. 79 eruption of Mt. Vesuvius.

"The excavated building, which has been identified as a gladiators' barracks since it contains paintings, *graffiti*, and inscriptions relating to their activities, was presumably a training school as well. Nearly a hundred rooms were grouped round a rectangular space of some 53 by 42 meters. Some of them were on an upper floor, reached by a staircase leading up to a wooden gallery, of which part has now been reconstructed. The cells on the two floors are between three and four meters square, without windows; these were the grim, dark, and dank quarters in which gladiators had to live. On their premises at Pompeii were found sixty-three skeletons of people who lost their lives in the eruption of Vesuvius."

The remains of the gladiator barracks at Pompeii, with its large rectangular training ground. Part of the perimeter was originally two stories high.

Ludus Matutinus—trained the hunters who fought wild animals in the amphitheaters.) The emperor Domitian began construction on the *Ludus Magnus* in the late first century, and Hadrian completed it a few decades later. The school was located near the Colosseum, and the two structures were conveniently connected by an underground tunnel. Imperial barracks also existed outside the capital in all of the provinces. Usually, the best fighters from these outlying areas were eventually summoned to perform in Rome before the emperor, whose *munera* were the largest and most prestigious.

Whichever *ludus* a recruit ended up in, his initial induction ceremony was the same. It consisted of swearing the gladiatorial oath, which probably went something like this: "I swear to be burned, to be bound, to be beaten, and to die by the sword." The exact words and the nature of other aspects of the ceremony, if any, are not certain. What little is known about the oath comes from paraphrases of it in the works of a small handful of ancient writers. Seneca the Younger, for instance, mentioned it in one of his letters. The Roman novelist Petronius also toys with the oath in his famous *Satyricon,* in which three unscrupulous young men get involved in adventures while traveling through southern Italy. At one point, the youths pretend they are the slaves of another man, Eumolpus, and they mimic gladiators swearing loyalty to a *lanista* or *procurator.* "To safeguard the imposture [charade] in which we were all involved," the narrator says,

> we swore an oath dictated by Eumolpus, that we would be burned, flogged, beaten, killed with cold steel or whatever else Eumolpus ordered. Like real gladiators we very solemnly handed ourselves over, body and soul, to our master. After swearing the oath, we saluted our master in our role as slaves.[23]

Indeed, in swearing the oath, a gladiator placed his body and soul in the hands of his *lanista* or *procurator.* By extension, he was also under the power of the emperor, games magistrate, and the spectators, all of them the gladiator's "betters." From then on, they possessed the moral authority to decide the gladiator's fate, ordering that he be either slain or spared according to their whims.

Life in a Gladiator Barracks

Not surprisingly, considering the brutality of the gladiator's profession, life in a gladiator barracks was monotonous, physically demanding, and generally uncompromising. The living quarters for the recruits were cold, spare, and grim. Roland Auguet, a noted expert on Roman spectacles, describes the gladiatorial living quarters at Pompeii, which are still partially intact thanks to the preservative effects of Mt. Vesuvius's ash. The school housed the recruits, he says,

> in rows of cells, some without skylights, which lined the square where they exercised. It was a prison, or at least the most forbidding of barracks. . . . The cells, ranged on two levels, were four yards long and without means of inter-communication. An immense kitchen, the far wall of which had a kitchen-range [hearth for cooking] along its whole length, occupied the center of one of the sides of the rectangle [central square]; there was a prison, in the exact sense of the term, and an armory.[24]

Inside the prison of this school (and presumably other gladiator schools across the Empire), the ceiling was so low that the inmates could only sit or lie down. They were shackled in sturdy and surely painful leg irons. This, and

This modern reenactment demonstrates how trainee gladiators practiced by circling and striking a wooden pole called a palus.

other evidence, illustrates that the *procuratores* who ran the gladiator schools maintained strict and harsh discipline, which is hardly surprising considering that each had to control hundreds of strong, tough men, most of whom did not want to be there. Such control obviously could not be maintained if the inmates had access to weapons when they were away from the training fields. So, there was a strict ban on weapons in the living quarters. Any breach of this ban could cause the *procurator* unwanted problems—perhaps a fine, punishment, or the loss of his job if an inmate killed himself or a trainer or, even worse, escaped.

Relentless Drills

Assuming they did not escape, and most did not, the gladiatorial recruits underwent a comprehensive and rigorous course of training. The instructors (*doctores*) were highly specialized, each an expert in some kind of weaponry or style of fighting. The *doctor thracicum,* for example, knew the ins and outs of fighting with the curved Thracian short sword, the *pica.* It comes as no surprise that

the majority of these teachers were former gladiators who had grown too old to fight and either could not or did not care to seek a life outside the profession.

The seemingly relentless drills supervised by these instructors took place in the school's rectangular central yard, where armed guards standing on the perimeter watched the trainees carefully. The *doctores* yelled various orders (*dictata*) at the recruits, making sure their footwork, lunges, parries, feints, and other moves were executed correctly. At this stage, much of a trainee's time was spent attacking a stationary six-foot-tall wooden pole, the *palus,* which represented an opponent. Sometimes the pole was rigged with hanging weights; when a man dodged one weight, the pole swung around, threatening him with a strike by another weight and forcing him to dodge again. Other times, the trainee used a wooden sword (*rudis*) to strike at the pole. Such drills helped develop better reflexes and hand-eye coordination, which were essential to success in combat. Occasionally the gladiator schools produced fighters with extraordinary visual acuity and reflexes. According to Pliny the Elder, "In the emperor Caligula's school for gladiators, there were 20,000 in training, of whom there were only two who did not blink when they faced some threat of danger; they were invincible."[25]

The training pole also lent its name to various teams or squads of gladiators in the school. Once the trainees reached a certain level of efficiency, each team, or *palus,* regularly squared off against the others in what might be described as in-house scrimmages. This approach, comments Harvard University scholar Kathleen Coleman, "would have supplied an excellent mechanism for encouraging competitive rivalry and objectifying [diminishing the personal stature of] the opposition."[26] The most skilled, respected, and envied team in a school was called the *primus palus,* the second-best the *secundus palus,* and so forth.

Learning Basic Tactics

Whichever group the recruits belonged to, and no matter what weapons and fighting style they would eventually adopt, all received instruction in certain basic tactics. After mastering the drills with the *palus* in the practice yard, they paired off and fought man to man, at first with wooden swords and later perhaps with blunt metal swords. (Several metal swords were discovered on the site of the gladiator school at Pompeii and may have been used in training; however, some scholars believe that the swords belonged to ornamental statues of gladiators and were never actually used by the trainees.)

Using their training swords and shields, the gladiators learned all the basic moves of attack and defense, including the so-called classic stance. This tactic was generally executed by combatants holding the standard rectangular shield (*scutum*) and stabbing sword (*gladius*), although it could be adapted and modified by fighters with different sorts of equipment. According to Graham Ashford, a reenactor who has closely studied and reconstructed ancient gladiatorial fights, the key to making the maneuver effective was to take full advantage of the cover provided by the shield. One formed the classic stance, Ashford writes,

by pulling the shield lightly against the left leg and left arm of the body, while the shield [was] held almost flat across the body. The right leg [was] used to support

Members of a modern reenactor group reconstruct a gladiator training session, each using a wooden sword (the rudis), *as real gladiators did.*

the stance from the rear with the weight distributed evenly across both feet when static. As much as [was] possible the shield [needed] to have three points of contact with the body, otherwise its size [could] prove counter-productive and easily unbalanced when under attack. The right arm [was] kept behind the shield with either the front end of the sword facing out to the enemy or hidden behind the shield to hide the sword's full length and position.[27]

At this point, the fighters were still a good distance apart and neither could reach the other with his weapon. They used this opportunity to "gain the measure of each other," Ashford explains, and held their shields upright so that "the enemy and weapons [were] hidden behind them."[28] This way a fighter's opponent could not see enough to predict what move he was planning.

When the time was right, one fighter advanced toward the other by taking a few short steps. The attacker was careful to keep his upper body tight and protected against the inside of the shield; he also positioned his sword arm behind the shield to keep his opponent from deflecting the weapon or wounding the arm. As the attacker moved in for the kill, Ashford continues,

> The position of the body to the shield [was] pivotal. By holding the *scutum* slightly above shoulder height, the gladiator [was] not only able to see everything that his enemy [was] doing while hiding much of his own movements. Also, he [could] defend his shoulders without any movement at all. . . . By being correctly positioned within the [protective curve of the] shield, attacks from the side . . . [could] be easily avoided, as the side of the shield pushed the blade past the back and sides or in the worst case

relegated a potentially lethal blow to a painful one. . . . In many [ancient painted and sculpted] gladiatorial images, the fight is all but lost because of the incorrect position of the *scutum,* which has left a side or arm uncovered. Wounds to these locations often resulted in the eventual defeat of the injured gladiator as exhaustion [was] quick to follow.[29]

Grim Realities of a Gladiator's Life

During these mock battles, many, if not most, of the trainees must have suffered minor injuries from time to time. In this regard, they had little to worry about. Amid all the confinement, harsh discipline, and relentless and demanding physical drills, which might seem inhumane by modern standards, the *procurator's* medical staff paid close attention to the health of the inmates. After all, these fighters

Another view of modern gladiator reenactors shows two trainees with wooden swords grappling for advantage.

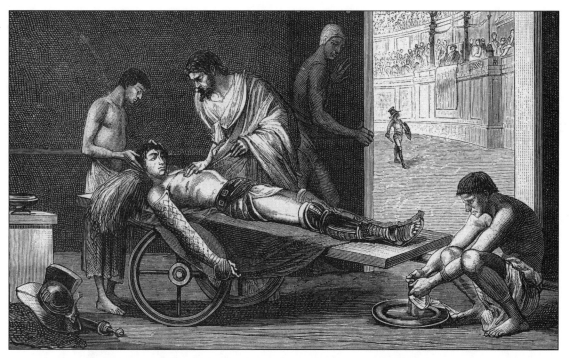

Gladiators usually had the benefit of excellent doctors. Here, the famous Greek physician Galen attends a badly wounded arena fighter.

were a valuable capital investment that needed to be protected, at least physically speaking. The *ludi,* Michael Grant states,

> were judiciously situated in favorable climates, and equipped with first-class doctors. Indeed, in the second century A.D. one of the most famous medical men of all time, Galen of Pergamum . . . served as a gladiators' doctor in his native Asia Minor . . . before rising to the position of [emperor] Marcus Aurelius's personal physician. When he was working with these fighters, Galen claimed that his attention to their health and horrible wounds was responsible for a substantial reduction of mortality. The schools were also provided with resident medical consultants to check the men's diet. . . . Inscriptions also record the services of skilled masseurs (*unctores*).[30]

As the date of a recruit's first amphitheater fight approached, he must have hoped that his months of weapons training and physical regimen had prepared him well for the few moments he would spend in the arena. The grim reality was that if he did not train hard enough and lacked proper preparation, he might well end up as a corpse lying in the blood-soaked sand.

Another grim reality of such combats was psychological in nature. When a gladiator won his match in the arena, the man he had managed to kill was often one of his barracks mates, someone he may have gotten to know during many months of training and sharing meals and perhaps conversation. "The entire notion of training amongst one's fellows in order to fight them in bloody public combat is riddled with paradox [something seemingly contradictory, yet true]," Kathleen Coleman suggests.

Combat at a Gladiator School Captured on Film

Probably the single most impressive and exciting modern cinematic staging of a gladiator fight appeared in the 1960 film *Spartacus*, directed by Stanley Kubrick. The title character (played by Kirk Douglas, who also produced the film) is the real-life gladiator who led a huge slave rebellion against the Roman state in the first century B.C. Before escaping the gladiator school of Lentulus Batiatus, to which he was brought in chains, Spartacus is forced to fight a fellow trainee in the facility's small arena to gratify a group of Roman aristocrats who are visiting the school. In this skillfully choreographed bout, Spartacus is arrayed as a Thracian, with an exposed chest, small round shield (*parma*), and curved sword (*sica*), while his opponent is a *retiarius*, with net and trident. Although the other man defeats Spartacus in the duel, he refuses to slay the fallen man when commanded to do so. For this display of insolence, the victor loses his own life, leaving the surprised Spartacus to ponder this noble act of courage and humanity. The scene effectively and movingly re-creates the spectacle, excitement, and brutality of the Roman arena, as well as the human side of gladiators and their lives.

Spartacus (played by Kirk Douglas) faces a fellow trainee in a duel to the death in the famous gladiatorial bout from Stanley Kubrick's epic film, Spartacus.

How could one go to work knowing that one might kill one's mess-mate today? The clue is in the word "work." Fighting was the gladiator's professional duty, whatever the results. It was a job; the gladiator had to do it; and it required a cool rationality, a fundamentally dispassionate attitude. . . . Yet one would expect that men living and training in a gladiatorial barracks in an almost tribal brotherhood would develop bonds that it would have been emotionally excruciating [painful] for them to violate. . . . [However,] given that gladiators originated in many different provinces of the Empire, they may not even have had a common language. There would also have been a constant turnover, with new recruits arriving, and some of the old hands away . . . doing the rounds of the local arenas. [31]

This was one of the sadder aspects of a gladiator's unenviable life: He was sometimes forced to kill someone he cared about and then to harden himself to the loss so that he could get past it emotionally and try to survive the next battle.

Many and Diverse Types of Arena Fighters

The first known type of gladiator, the Samnite, dating from the late fourth century B.C., proved to be popular for centuries with the crowds that attended Rome's amphitheater games. If this had remained the only kind of arena fighter, the *munera* would have been much less varied and colorful. As it was, though, several different types or categories of gladiators developed during the late Republic and early Empire. Each type had its own distinctive armor (or lack thereof), weapons, and fighting style, and each represented a typical warrior of a foreign people, usually one that had fought and been defeated by Rome.

The *munera,* therefore, became more than just entertainment. These games were also a form of propaganda, as well as a venue for Romans to express their nationalism and pride in their forefathers' accomplishments. Those foreign armies foolhardy enough to challenge invincible Rome were in the arena symbolically reduced to miserable captives forced to fight one another to the death before their Roman "betters."

The Samnite and His Offspring

The exact number and kinds of gladiators are uncertain and disputed by scholars. There may have been as many as fifteen, twenty, or more distinctive types. Or there may have been as few as six or seven kinds, each having minor variations that in modern times have been mistaken for separate types of fighters.

The original gladiator type, the Samnite, and its possible spin-offs are a case in point. The gladiators referred to as the *hoplomachus*

The gladiator known as the Samnite was based on the look of actual Samnite warriors.

and *secutor* may have been later forms or variations of the Samnite. It is certainly possible that the Romans recognized these three as separate and distinct types, but any major distinctions are now unclear, since all employed basically the same weapons and tactics. They each carried a sword and shield and wore a metal helmet and protective armor on one leg (or perhaps occasionally both legs). According to Roland Auguet,

> The kinship of their weapons is evident. It is that of the ordinary [Roman] infantryman [whose equipment was borrowed in large degree from Samnite warriors]. . . . This kinship is further explained by the fact that they were related by descent. It is noticeable that the Samnite, formerly frequently mentioned in the [ancient] texts, is no longer mentioned after the first days of the Empire, a period in which, on the contrary, the *hoplomachus* and the *secutor* first appear. We must therefore conclude . . . that this disappearance was due to some specialization of which the precise nature has escaped us, as it has of course in the case of most of the details which differentiated these three categories.[32]

Some scholars contend that the differences between these gladiator types may not have been as minor as Auguet says. Some point to evidence suggesting that the *hoplomachus* carried a round shield (as opposed to the rectangular *scutum* held by the Samnite and *secutor*) and perhaps also a spear in addition to his sword. This might mean that the *hoplomachus* was based on the Greek hoplite, a heavily armored infantry soldier whose principal weapon was the spear and secondary one the sword. It has also been suggested that the *secutor* wore a helmet that was more rounded and protective of the face than a Samnite helmet. Whether this distinction alone was enough to classify the *secutor* as a completely separate gladiator type is unknown.

Another gladiator type that bore a resemblance to the Samnite and *secutor* was the

This exquisite Roman mosaic found at Lepcis Magna (in North Africa) shows various kinds of gladiators, including a retiarius *(at far left), a Samnite, and various types similar to the Samnite. The man at far right is a referee.*

myrmillo, or "fishman," named after the *mormylos,* a sea-fish represented in a prominent crest on his helmet. Like the Samnite and *secutor,* the *myrmillo* carried a rectangular shield. However, evidence suggests that the *myrmillo* was less heavily armored than these other types, perhaps having no other protection than his shield and helmet (and perhaps a single greave, a lower-leg protector, usually made of bronze).

Various ancient writers mention *myrmillones* in situations both in and out of the arena. One of the more notorious appears in Suetonius's biography of the third emperor, Caligula (Gaius Caesar). The vain and twisted Caligula went to an imperial gladiator school and insisted on engaging a *myrmillo* in a sparring match with wooden swords (the kind with which the gladiators trained). Unfortunately for the gladiator, he made the mistake of thinking that if he allowed the emperor to win, he would be satisfied and go away. But the brutal Caligula took advantage of the man when he was down. According to Suetonius,

> On another occasion a gladiator from the school against whom he [Caligula] was fencing with a wooden sword fell down deliberately; whereupon Gaius drew a real dagger, stabbed him to death, and ran about waving the palm-branch of victory. [33]

The Thracian and *Retiarius*

Like the *myrmillo*, the Thracian, another distinct gladiator type, was relatively lightly armored. The Thracian was so named because he resembled fighters from Thrace, a region of northern Greece. The Thracian wielded a curved short sword, the *sica,* and a small round shield, the *parma.* His legs were protected by *fasciae,* strips of leather wound around the thighs, and greaves.

While the Thracian wore little armor, another common kind of gladiator, the *retiarius,* or "net man," wore no armor at all. A *retiarius* attempted to ensnare his opponent in his net (or used the net to trip the other man) and then stab him with a long, razor-sharp trident, a three-pronged spear. Historian Stephen Wisdom writes,

> *Retiarii* were usually handsome young men; the average age of a gladiator was between 18 and 25, although one was still fighting as late as his 40s. With minimal combat equipment, [*retiarii*] used the 1.6m (5 1/4 ft) trident or harpoon, the *fascina,* and a small dagger, the *pugio. Retiarii* were also equipped with a 3m (9ft 9in) diameter net, the *rete,* with which they could ensnare opponents, trip them, or whip them. The weights were like modern fishing weights and if lashed with sufficient power, the net could blind a man. Around the perimeter of the net was a rope, both ends of which were tied to the wrist of the *retiarius.* If thrown unnecessarily, he could jerk the net back into his grip. However, if the net was caught by his opponent and used to pull the *retiarius* off balance, then he could use the dagger to cut himself free. Without his net . . . [his] trident held in both hands became an effective weapon. [34]

For reasons that are unclear today, the *retiarius* did not generally possess the same status or command the same respect as most other gladiators. He was assigned the poorest living quarters in gladiator schools, for example. Some scholars suggest that this stemmed from his lack of armor. In the Roman mindset, shaped by centuries of idolizing heavily armored legionnaires (army infantrymen), armor may have been equated with manliness; thus, naked flesh in place of armor (as in the case of the *retiarius*) may have seemed unmanly. Also, out of necessity (because of his lack of armor), the *retiarius* tended to back away or even run from an opponent if he lost both his net and trident. Any sort of retreat was also viewed as unmanly. Whatever the reasons that the *retiarius* occupied a low position in the gladiatorial pecking order, what is certain is that some ancient writers poked fun at this gladiator type. In one of his satires, Juvenal has harsh words for a descendant of one of Rome's noblest families who decided to volunteer as a *retiarius:*

The games! Go there for the ultimate scandal. Look at Gracchus who fights, but not with the arms of a swordsman, not with a dagger or shield (he hates and despises such weapons), nor does a helmet hide his face. What he holds is a trident. What he hurls is a net, and he misses, of course, and we see him look up at the seats, then run for his life, all around the arena, easy for all to know and identify. Look at his tunic, golden cord and fringe, and that queer conspicuous arm guard![35]

A Thracian *has become entangled in the net of a* retiarius, *who now threatens with his trident, in this memorable scene from Guazzoni's* Messalina.

An Awesome Display of Fighting Prowess

Unfortunately, few film depictions of ancient Roman gladiatorial combats have been accurately costumed or staged. One of the few notable exceptions was *Demetrius and the Gladiators* (1954, directed by Delmer Davies). The title character (played by Victor Mature) is a former Greek slave condemned to train at a gladiator school in Rome. At first, because he is a Christian, he refuses to kill. But when he believes that one of his friends has been slain by a gladiator, he changes his mind. Armed as a *myrmillo* (or *hoplomachus*), with helmet, sword, and shield, he fights and defeats a *retiarius*, armed with net and trident, in an exhibition before the corrupt emperor Caligula. Seconds later, Demetrius defeats three other opponents sent against him simultaneously in a skillfully staged, well-filmed, and truly exciting arena battle.

This scene may have been loosely based on a real incident mentioned by the Roman historian Suetonius in his biography of Caligula (part of his *Lives of the Twelve Caesars*). Two groups of fighters, says Suetonius, one made up of "net-and-trident gladiators [*retiarii*]," the other of "men-at-arms [*secutores*]," squared off. The emperor sentenced the net fighters to death, prompting one of them to grab a trident and kill "each of the victorious team in turn." Caligula's response to this awesome display of individual fighting prowess, one rarely seen in the arena, was to call it "murder."

In an early scene from Demetrius, *the title character refuses to slay his fallen opponent. Demetrius is arrayed as a* myrmillo, *although his two greaves and round shield belong to a* hoplomachus.

Apparently, though, it was not always the *retiarius* who ended up running away during combat. Most Romans were familiar with a popular tale regarding the traditional rivalry between *myrmillones* and *retiarii*. Supposedly, a *myrmillo* retreated from a net man, who yelled, "It is not you I am trying to catch, it's your fish [a reference to the fish crest on the man's helmet]; why do you run away?"[36]

Some Offbeat Gladiator Types

Myrmillones were paired not only with *retiarii* but with Thracians. Another traditional opponent of a *retiarius* was the *secutor*. In addition to these and other standard pairings of the major gladiator types, several special and offbeat types and pairings were featured in the *munera*. Among these types was the *dimachaerius*, a gladiator who fought without a shield and wielded two swords (or daggers), one in each hand. Graham Ashford offers these insights based on his modern reconstructions of gladiatorial bouts:

In brief experiments of a matched pair consisting of a *scutarius* (large shield fighter, like a Samnite or *myrmillo*) against a *dimachaerius* it soon became obvious that the main strength of the *dimachaerius* lay in the ability to be able to rain down a series of quick blows which left the *scutarius* almost unable to consider a counter attack. At this stage . . . the counter attacks could be made but they were made blindly or with tremendous commitment, and consequently, peril to the *scutarius*. The main way of offense appears to be to confuse the enemy with volley after volley of swift slashes and thrusts until a mistake is made and the fatal blow can be delivered. The primary weakness of the *dimachaerius* seems to be [his] inability to defend at very close quarters; once the attack has been made by the *dimachaerius*, it becomes difficult to defend against thrusts to the stomach and lower chest due to the lack of a shield that would otherwise passively resist the attack.[37]

Even more unusual than the *dimachaerius* was another minor gladiator type, the *laquearius*. The main offensive weapon of the *laquearius* was a lasso, with which, it appears, he tripped or entangled an opponent and then choked him (or perhaps finished him off with a dagger). Lassos were also used by *equites*, gladiators who fought on horseback. These fighters, about whom very little is known, also wielded lances and/or swords.

Other gladiators who were associated with horses—the *essedarii*—fought their opponents from moving chariots, which was apparently a Celtic style of fighting introduced to the *munera* after Julius Caesar's conquest of Gaul. (The Celts, whom the Romans viewed as "barbarians," inhabited a wide strip of northern Europe stretching from the southern Black Sea region in the east to Britain and Ireland in the west. The Romans called those Celts living in what is now France "Gauls.") Petronius mentions an *essedarius*, interestingly a female one, in his *Satyricon*. A merchant attending a sumptuous banquet speaks about an upcoming gladiatorial show, saying,

We'll be having a holiday with a three-day show that's the best ever—and not just a hack troupe of [slave] gladiators but freedmen [freed slaves, who enjoyed a higher status than slaves]. [The person giving the games] will give us cold steel, no quarter [i.e., no sparing of the fighters' lives], and the slaughterhouse right in the middle [of

The opening moments of a battle between essedarii *may have looked like this. However, some scholars think these fighters eventually dismounted and fought on foot.*

the amphitheater]. . . . He's got some big brutes already, and a woman who fights in a chariot. [38]

Brief references to *essedarii* also appear in the works of the Roman humorist Martial and some inscriptions. However, a number of scholars think that such references are misleading. In their view, these chariot-driving warriors were less likely full-fledged gladiators who fought in the *munera* and more likely animal fighters who took part in the wild beast hunts that accompanied the gladiatorial bouts.

Perhaps the most bizarre of the gladiators about whom any significant information has survived were the *andabates,* who grappled while blindfolded by massive helmets with no eyeholes. One would suppose that these fighters must have groped around, swinging their weapons to and fro in hopes of killing an opponent with a lucky blow. However, luck "played little part in the outcome of the combat," Auguet writes.

A coat of mail [armor] covered the [*andabate's*] whole body, so that the blows which the gladiator beating the air with his sword chanced to land were harmless instead of mortal. In order to deceive his adversary, the *andabate* might well maneuver in the arena with all the precautions of a skin-diver in deep water anxious not to scare the fish; but it was not trickery any more than luck, but skill in swordsmanship and strength which were finally the decisive factors of victory, since the sole method of winning was to strike at the joints of the [armor]. The training which they received at the barracks turned them not merely into good gladiators but also into good players of blind man's bluff. [39]

Still other minor types of gladiators are mentioned in inscriptions, but almost nothing is known about them except for their names. One of the most intriguing are the *scissors,* which means "carvers"; one wonders if this nickname referred to the weapons they used (perhaps a special kind of sword or dagger?) or to their peculiar and probably gruesome technique of dispatching their opponents.

More General Designations of Gladiators

In addition to specific gladiator types, more general designations were given to gladiators based on the ways they were paired or their status. For example, most of the time gladiators fought in pairs, one fighter against another. Regardless of their individual type (*myrmillo, retiarius,* Thracian, and so forth), all gladiators who fought in pairs were referred to as *ordinarii,* or "ordinary gladiators." On the less frequent occasions when larger numbers fought, usually one team against another, they were called *catervarii,* or "group fighters." Suetonius describes such a bout in his tract on Caligula:

A group of net-and-trident gladiators [*retiarii*], dressed in tunics, put up a very poor show against the five men-at-arms [*secutores*] with whom they were matched; but when he [Caligula] sentenced them to death, one of them seized a trident and killed each of the victorious team in turn. [The emperor] then publicly expressed his horror at what he called "this most bloody murder," and his disgust with those who had been able to stomach the fight. [40]

Another designation of gladiators that applied regardless of their types was *postulaticii,* meaning "requested" or "demanded" gladiators. Their name derived from those occasions when a crowd called on the games magistrate to bring out some fighters who had not been listed on the regular program. In addition,

The Emperor's Favorite Gladiator

The Flavian emperor Domitian, son of Vespasian and brother of Titus, was a huge fan of the *munera.* Domitian especially liked to watch women fight in the arena, and among male gladiators, he particularly disliked Thracians. The emperor had a strong preference for the *myrmillones* and could become quite angry with anyone who made a disparaging remark about his favorites. According to Suetonius in his biography of Domitian (in *The Twelve Caesars*), one day when the emperor was attending a bout at the recently constructed Colosseum, a *myrmillo* and a Thracian were engaged in combat. Suetonius writes,

"A chance remark by one citizen, to the effect that a Thracian gladiator might be 'a match for his Gallic opponent [a *myrmillo* was a Gallic-type gladiator], but not for the patron of the games [i.e., Domitian himself],' was enough to have him dragged from his seat and—with a placard tied around his neck reading: 'A Thracian supporter who spoke disloyally'—torn to pieces by dogs in the arena."

gladiators of all types who managed to survive the arena long enough to retire were called *rudiarii.* The name came from *rudis,* the wooden sword with which gladiators trained and which they received as a ceremonial gift on leaving the profession. Not surprisingly, such veterans were usually top-notch fighters and many spectators were sorry to see them go. For the right price, though, they could be coaxed into returning briefly, as Suetonius relates in his biography of the second emperor, Tiberius:

> He staged a gladiatorial contest in memory of his father . . . and another in memory of his grandfather. . . . The first took place in the Forum, the second in the amphitheater [of Taurus]; and he persuaded some retired gladiators to appear with the rest, by paying them 1,000 gold pieces each. [41]

The Gladiatrix

So far, the focus has been mainly on male gladiators—and for good reason. The fact is that the vast majority of gladiators were men. However, as Petronius's reference to a female *essedarius* shows, some cases of women gladiators and other arena fighters are known. Certain emperors liked them more than others; for example, Domitian enjoyed pitting women not only against other women but also against male dwarves.

It is unclear whether these women fought only in the standard outfits and styles used by their male counterparts or whether a few specialized female gladiator types existed as well. It is known that women gladiators adopted stage names, much as modern professional wrestlers do. Two mentioned in ancient inscriptions are

A huge brawl erupts among catervarii *(gladiators who fought in groups) in this scene from the 1935 film version of* The Last Days of Pompeii.

Female gladiators were often associated in art and literature with the Amazons, a tribe of warrior women from Greek mythology. This modern sculpture depicts an Amazon spearing a lion.

Achillia, a feminine form of Achilles, the warrior hero of Homer's *Iliad,* and Amazon, a reference to the famous race of warrior women in Greek mythology.

More emerges from the comparison of women gladiators to Amazons than simply a borrowed name. The Greeks and Romans viewed the legendary Amazons in a negative light, seeing them as unnatural, uncontrolled, barbaric forces that posed a potential threat to traditional male-dominated society. Women were expected to know their place, a decidedly subordinate one, in that society. And to call a woman an Amazon was an insult. Since even male gladiators were widely seen as low-life, most people viewed the female gladiator, or "gladiatrix," as especially scandalous. Juvenal, whose satires ridiculed so many other aspects of society, was unusually hard on women gladiators:

And what about female athletes, with their purple track-suits, and wrestling in the mud? Not to mention our lady-fencers [sword fighters]. We've all seen *them,* stabbing the stump with a foil [sword], shield well advanced, going through the proper motions. Just the right training needed to blow a matronly horn at the Floral Festival [held in late April and early May; all Roman festivals began with trumpet volleys] —unless they have higher ambitions, and the goal of all their practice is the real arena. But then, what modesty can be looked for in some helmeted vixen, a renegade from her sex, who thrives on masculine violence—yet would not prefer to *be* a man, since the pleasure is so much less? What a fine sight for some husband—*it might be you*—his wife's equipment put up

Evidence for Women Gladiators

In the following excerpt from an article in *Ludus Gladiatorius,* an online study of Roman arena fighters, researcher Graham Ashford summarizes some of the existing evidence for women gladiators.

The bones in the dishes were found in 1996 and are thought to be the remains of a gladiatrix.

"A foremost [surviving] piece of archaeology [relating to] female gladiators . . . comes from Halicarnassus [a Greek city on what is now the western coast of Turkey], [and is] currently held in the British Museum. The stone shows two female fighters with their names, 'Amazonia and Achillea,' included with the two helmetless fighters. They stand opposite one another armed with swords and crouched behind *scuta* [rectangular shields]. At their feet are either their helmets or the head and shoulders of the watching crowd. The inscription with them tells us that they were both allowed to walk free from the arena, presumably as a reward of their fighting ability, although other possibilities present themselves. . . . Of all the scant information left us about female gladiators, this is one of the most compelling as it shows they fought against other female fighters and were taken seriously enough to have a large stone carved in their honor."

at auction, sword-belt, armlet, plumes [helmet decorations], and one odd shinguard! Or, if the other style of fighting takes her fancy, imagine your delight when the dear girl sells off her greaves! . . . Note how she snorts at each practice thrust, bowed down by the weight of her helmet . . . then wait for the laugh, when she lays down her weapons and squats over the potty![42]

It was bad enough for a woman of slave or other lower-class status to appear in the arena. But for an upper-class lady to do so was seen as especially revolting and disreputable. According to Tacitus, the ninth year of Nero's

reign (A.D. 63) "witnessed gladiatorial displays on a no less magnificent scale than before, but exceeding all precedent in the number of distinguished women and senators disgracing themselves in the arena."[43] It must be pointed out, however, that the cruel Nero likely forced most or all of these well-to-do persons to fight, so these women were probably not professional gladiators.

Eventually, the gladiatrix disappeared from the Roman arena. In the early third century, the emperor Septimius Severus decided to ban female combatants from the amphitheater games. Perhaps he thought that professional killing, in both the army and the arena, was better left to the men.

Hunters and Beast Men

Besides the various kinds of male and female gladiators, the amphitheater games featured another kind of arena fighter—the "hunter," or *venator*. Some arena hunters were also called *bestiarii*, meaning "beast men." The two labels may have been more or less interchangeable; however, a number of scholars think the term *bestiarii* referred to lower-status hunters or people condemned to be killed by beasts. It may have also denoted hunters who employed a different fighting style than the *venatores*.

What is more certain is that the arena hunters resembled gladiators in many ways. Like gladiators, most *venatores* began as slaves and criminals, but a few were probably free-born volunteers. They trained in a specialized school—the *ludus bestiariorum*—which was very similar to a gladiator barracks. The main difference may have been that the hunters received somewhat less comprehensive and rigorous training than gladiators did, although this is by no means certain.

An arena hunter's standard weapon was a spear with an iron-reinforced point—the *venabulum*. However, the hunters used a number of

The term bestiarii *may refer to individuals who were condemned to fight to the death against wild animals, as depicted in this old engraving.*

other weapons, too, among them swords, daggers, clubs, and bows and arrows. Those hunters who specialized in killing with the bow were called *sagitarii*. In addition, some hunters specialized in killing only one kind of animal; for example, the *taurarii* squared off with bulls and tried to stab them with lances, much like modern matadors. In an exciting variation of this event, a hunter jumped from horseback onto the bull, grabbed its horns, and tried to wrestle it to the ground before killing it. Except for the hunter's costume, this performance was probably nearly identical to its counterpart in modern rodeos.

Another way the arena hunters resembled gladiators was how they won the adulation and allegiance of the spectators. Surviving evidence shows that the most successful, colorful, and

A lion attacks a mounted venator in this fanciful modern rendering. Some arena hunters used spears and lances, others swords, ropes, and bows and arrows.

The violence of the gladiatorial combats occasionally spilled over into the audience, as shown in this excerpt from Tacitus's *Annals* documenting a serious riot that occurred in Pompeii's arena in A.D. 59, during Nero's reign.

"There was a serious fight between the inhabitants of two [neighboring] Roman settlements, Nuceria and Pompeii. It arose out of a trifling incident at a gladiatorial show given by Livineius Regulus. . . . During an exchange of taunts—characteristic of these disorderly country towns—abuse led to stone-throwing, and then swords were drawn. The people of Pompeii, where the show was held, came off best. Many wounded and mutilated Nucerians were taken to the capital [Rome]. Many bereavements, too, were suffered by parents and children. The emperor instructed the Senate to investigate the affair. The Senate passed it to the consuls. When they reported back, the Senate debarred Pompeii from holding any similar gathering for ten years. Illegal associations in the town were dissolved; and the sponsor of the show and his fellow instigators of the disorders were exiled."

entertaining hunters became almost as popular with the public as winning gladiators. One of the most widely acclaimed of all the *venatores* was a man named Carpophorus, who gained fame in the arena during Domitian's reign. In one of several epigrams dedicated to Carpophorus, Martial writes,

He plunged his spear also in a charging bear, once prime in the peak of the Arctic pole [possibly a reference to a polar bear]; he laid low a lion of unprecedented size, a sight to see, who might have done honor to Hercules' hands [the mythical character Hercules was credited with slaying the powerful Nemean lion]; he stretched dead a fleet leopard with a wound felt from afar. [44]

In addition to their entertainment value, hunters like Carpophorus and the animals they dispatched had an added political dimension, just as gladiators did. After conquering various lands and territories, the Romans began importing animals native to those regions for use in the amphitheaters. So, the spectators came to associate the animals they saw in specific shows with the regions in which these beasts were captured. This was a constant and potent reminder that Rome had overpowered and remained master of those regions. As scholar Richard C. Beacham puts it, the hunters and their prey

encouraged the spectators to associate military prowess and the geographic expansion of Roman influence with various animals from the distant realms subject to Roman might. Through the display of such exotic booty, power was rendered both graphic and entertaining. [45]

Death in the Arena: Gladiators in Action

Nearly the entire life of a gladiator was strictly regimented, with rules and routines imposed by others. On reaching the barracks, he recited his oath when told to, then drilled, ate, and slept on command. He could not go anywhere else, do anything else, or associate with anyone else unless his keepers and handlers said he could.

Likewise, when the gladiator finally walked into the center of an amphitheater to fight, the show in which he took part was highly regimented and formalized, a public ceremony tightly scripted by tradition, custom, and accepted rules of conduct. The gladiator and his opponent entered the arena at a prescribed time; at a given signal, they went through the preliminary rituals; at another signal, they started fighting; and the survivor (or both if it was a draw) walked out of the arena precisely when and where ordered to do so. No deviations from these procedures, or any sort of protests or appeals for leniency, were possible. Such insolence would have led to almost immediate execution.

In addition, during his brief moment in the public spotlight, the gladiator had the obligation not only to perform but to perform well. Appeasing and pleasing the spectators, espe-

A Spectacular Film Riddled with Errors

Unfortunately, although the film *Gladiator* (released in 2000) was spectacular and well acted, its depictions of gladiators and their combats were frequently inaccurate. Two noted scholars of ancient Rome here weigh in on the subject. Robert B. Kebric, of the University of Louisville (from the manuscript of a forthcoming book about the film), writes,

"The treatment of gladiators in *Gladiator* is stereotypical, superficial, and the gladiatorial combat in the movie is mostly show and effect. Contests looked more like 'free for alls' with everyone, no matter what their level of skill, fighting everyone else to the death. Some of the combatants show up in outrageous, totally impractical costumes. From what appears in *Gladiator,* one could never distinguish differences between the unskilled masses of condemned criminals and prisoners of war made to fight as gladiators, and the select, elevated, highly visible trained career professionals."

University of Connecticut scholar Allen Ward agrees, writing (in an article for the *New England Classical News Letter*),

"The depiction of gladiatorial armor, weapons, and combat in *Gladiator* is riddled with errors. . . . True gladiatorial combats were not the kind of mass melees often shown in the movie, but individual duels fought under strict rules enforced by referees."

cially the emperor or other authority figure present, was as important as defeating one's opponent. If the audience deemed a gladiator's performance somehow substandard, he could be beaten or even killed. After all, he had earlier sworn an oath to fight and die for his "betters," and to break that oath would be to throw away the only badge of honor to which he could lay claim. Thus, the gladiator was trapped by circumstance and tradition and had no choice but to follow the amphitheater's rules and customs faithfully and to fight as vigorously and skillfully as he could.

Preliminary Arena Ceremonies

The first of the time-honored customs to be observed at the start of a typical *munus* was the *pompa,* a colorful parade in which the gladiators entered the arena. It was similar in some ways to the stately procession held on the opening day of the modern Olympic Games, though in addition to the athletes (if one can think of the gladiators as athletes), the *pompa* featured a number of nonathletes. Jugglers, acrobats, and other circus-like performers accompanied the gladiators, and all kept time to marching music played on trumpets, flutes, drums, and sometimes a large hydraulic organ. (The musicians probably also played during the actual fighting, producing an effect similar to that of the background musical score of a movie.)

At the conclusion of the *pompa,* the acrobats and other minor performers exited. Then the gladiators proceeded, in full public view, to draw lots, which decided how they would be paired in their combats. The games magistrate, or *munerarius,* supervised the drawing or drawings (there may have been a number of separate ones). It is probable, for example, that experienced veterans usually drew only against one another, for, as Roland Auguet points out,

A group of gladiators marches into an amphitheater during the pompa, *a colorful parade that preceded the matches.*

There would have been no point in opposing [matching up] a veteran . . . and some novice who had not yet had even a single victory. Furthermore, the gladiator himself would have judged it dishonorable to be paired with an adversary not of his stature.[46]

Once it had been decided who would fight whom, the *munerarius* (or on occasion some distinguished guest, or even the emperor himself) inspected the fighters' weapons to make sure they were sound and well sharpened. This process was called the *probatio armorum* (meaning the "approval," "proof," or "test" of arms). Like so many other customs of the

A retiarius fights a myrmillo *as the crowd cheers. The man on the horse behind them is a referee, who could interrupt the fight, call for a break, or discipline the fighters at his will.*

arena, it probably derived from some early solemn ceremony associated with funeral rituals. The last part of the preliminary arena ceremony consisted of a formal salute to the highest-ranking official present—if not the emperor, usually the *munerarius*. The gladiators soberly raised their weapons toward the official and recited the phrase *"Morituri te salutant!"* which means "Those about to die salute you!"

"Now He's Done For!"

After the salute, all of the gladiators exited, except for the two who had been selected to take part in the first arena battle. As for how they actually fought, no detailed, blow-by-blow description of such a combat has survived. However, a number of modern scholars and reenactors have managed to reconstruct many of the essential strategies, moves, and other elements of such bouts. The version excerpted below, by Auguet, depicting a confrontation between a *retiarius* and a *secutor,* is believable given the evidence and provides an idea of some of these elements, as well as the desperation and ferocity of the fighting:

> Apart from retreat, his [the *retiarius*'s] sole means of defense was attack; as soon as he had gained enough ground to turn without danger, he was once more on the attack, his body twisted slightly to the left by the trident which he thrust out before him, head down, to keep his adversary at a distance. In his right hand he balanced a net, which he swung round in a circular movement. But as soon as he had thrown it, his adversary ducked, raising the shield which he held in his left hand to the level of his eyes. . . . As soon as the dry rattle of the [net's] meshes against the metal had warned him that he was safe, [the *secutor*] counterattacked, sword in hand; but now the *retiarius* had no time to recover his net before running away. It was a first step towards defeat for, well thrown, his weapon could by itself decide the issue of combat. [47]

Having lost his net, the *retiarius* had no choice but to rely on his other principal weapon—the trident. He likely grasped it with both hands, Auguet suggests, holding the section of the shaft near the prongs with his left hand and the end of the shaft with his right one. For a while, the *retiarius* kept the *secutor* back by keeping the extended trident between his own body and his opponent's. Then, when he thought he saw an opening, Auguet continues,

> he attacked, thrusting the trident violently downward as if to pin a monster to the ground. . . . The *secutor* parried the blows with his sword rather than by using his shield. . . . He was trying to make it [the trident] fall from the hands of the *retiarius* and, with this in view, went so far as to use his shield as an offensive weapon; seizing the moment of an attack from below, he thrust it down on the inclined shaft, throwing his whole weight upon it, to make his adversary lose his grip. The latter, forced to draw aside to avoid the sword threatening his flank [side] . . . had great difficulty in breaking away. Parrying one of his adversary's blows on the left, he caught the *secutor*'s shield on the right and he succeeded in tearing it away; but, thrown off balance by the effort, the two men rolled on the ground and the trident flew several yards away. They did not think of recovering their arms but threw themselves on each other, crawling over the sand in a sort of duel with knives. At each movement the spectators . . . shouted in the ears of imaginary neighbors . . . "He's going to strike!", "He's missed!" [48]

Indeed, as Auguet points out, the audience played a major role in heightening the excitement of the combat, similar to what happens at modern boxing and wrestling matches. Among the common phrases screamed by the onlookers were *"Verbera!"* ("Strike!"), *"Habet!"* ("A hit!"), *"Hoc habet!"* ("Now he's done for!"), *"Ure!"* ("Burn him up!"), and *"Jugula!"* ("Cut his throat!").

Possible Outcomes of Combat

Regardless of the kinds of gladiators fighting or the strategies and moves they employed, there were several possible outcomes for any given match. The most common of these can be seen in surviving examples of the lists drawn up at the end of each *munus*. These lists consist of the fighters' names, followed by the appropriate letters, including P (for *periit*, "perished"), V (for *vicit*, "won"), or M (for *missus*, denoting a loser who was allowed to live and fight another day). Thus, a fighter could win either by killing his opponent outright or by decisively incapacitating him in some way.

In another possible outcome, when both warriors fought bravely and were unable to defeat each other, the *munerarius* might call the match a draw. In that case, each gladiator was described as *stans missus*. This must have been a fairly common outcome because it is mentioned frequently in ancient inscriptions. For example, the epitaph of a fighter named Flamma claims that in his thirty-eight bouts he won twenty-five times, was *missus* four times, and *stans missus* nine times. When each combatant was *stans missus*, prizes, in the form of palm branches and money, could be given to both or neither, depending on the situation. In an epigram meant to please his imperial patron, Domitian, Martial told about a draw that ended with both fighters receiving a prize:

The match depicted in this late nineteenth-century painting follows the rule of sine missione, *in which no draws are allowed. A victorious* retiarius *is about to dispatch his opponent.*

As Priscus and Verus each drew out the contest and the struggle between the pair long stood equal, shouts loud and often sought discharge for the combatants. But Caesar [a reference to Domitian, the name Caesar by now having become an imperial title] obeyed his own law (the law was that the bout go on without shield until a finger was raised [the signal from one fighter that he surrendered]). . . . But an end to the even strife was found: equal they fought, equal they yielded. To both, Caesar sent wooden swords [like those they had trained with, in this case symbolizing their discharge from service] and to both palms. Thus valor and skill had their reward. This has happened under no prince but you, Caesar: two fought and both won.[49]

By contrast, draws were not permitted in another, mercifully less common kind of combat—the *sine missione.* In this situation, the gladiators had to keep fighting, no matter how long it took, until one was killed. (Augustus banned this practice, thinking it cruel, but other emperors later revived it.)

There were still other possible outcomes of gladiatorial matches. For instance, in some cases both the officials and the spectators felt that the fighters were not giving it their all. In his *Satyricon,* Petronius has a character complain,

> What good has Norbanus [a politician who staged a gladiator show] done us? He put on some half-pint gladiators, so done-in already that they'd have dropped if you blew on them. I've seen animal killers [most of whom had less training than gladiators] fight better. . . . One boy did have a little spirit—he was in Thracian armor [i.e., carried a Thracian sword and

shield], and even he didn't show any initiative. In fact, they were all flogged afterwards [for failing to fight well], there were so many shouts of "Give 'em what for!" from the crowd. Pure yellow [cowardice], that's all.[50]

An even more disgraceful display was when one combatant simply turned and ran for his life. One of the surviving Pompeiian inscriptions says, "Officiosus fled on November 6 in the consulate of Drusus Caesar and M. Junius Norbanus."[51] It is unknown how often this happened, but when it did the offender was punished by whipping, branding with hot irons, or immediate execution.

Fate of the Fallen Fighter

Certainly one of the more fateful, anxious, and tense moments in an arena fight was when one gladiator went down wounded, which occurred quite often. The fallen contestant was allowed to raise one finger, which signified an appeal for mercy; otherwise, he was not permitted to move or especially to reach for his weapons. If he did have the audacity to seize a weapon and try to resume the battle, he immediately incurred the wrath of the highest-ranking official present as well as that of the crowd, which almost always booed and cursed him.

Such a display was extremely rare, however. The vast majority of fallen, wounded gladiators showed incredible discipline and courage by simply lying quietly and submitting to their fate. Usually, that fate was decided by the emperor or *munerarius,* often in accordance with the crowd's wishes. The traditional consensus among modern historians has been that if the spectators desired a fighter spared, they signaled their desire with a "thumbs up" gesture; if their choice was death, they indicated it with

In French artist Jean Gerome's great painting, Pollice Verso *("Thumb's Down"), a victorious gladiator awaits the life-and-death decision of the crowd.*

a "thumbs down." This may indeed be the case. However, several experts have offered other intriguing possibilities, such as a "thumbs down" (along with the waving of handkerchiefs) as the signal for the victor to drop his sword and spare the loser, and the pressing of the thumb toward the chest (symbolizing a sword through the heart) to call for death.

One can imagine another possible way for a fallen fighter to escape death—namely, if, instead of raising his finger in appeal, he pretended to be dead. However, it is hard to believe that anyone was ever successful at this charade. To guard against such a possibility, men dressed as ancient demons ran out and applied hot irons to the body or bodies lying in the arena. Any fakers exposed in this manner promptly had their throats cut.

Whether dispatched by his opponent or the amphitheater's attendants, when a gladiator finally lay dead in the sand, the arena had to be quickly prepared for the next set of combatants. Men dressed as the god Mercury (who, in addition to being a divine messenger, was the transporter of the dead to the Underworld) ran out and dragged away the corpse; then a team of young boys hurriedly cleaned the bloodstains from the sand.

Arena Executions

The bloody end of a gladiator's life was not the only form of death that occurred in the Roman arena. During the course of a typical amphitheater show, the gladiators not only fought and killed one another but also engaged in massacres of ordinary people who had been convicted of various crimes. The word massacre is indeed appropriate, since the condemned individuals were completely or almost completely defenseless. These killings were not part of the *munera* in the strict sense, and it is important to understand the distinction between formal gladiatorial fights, which involved trained fighters, and what were essentially public executions conducted by gladiators at the behest of the state.

It is perhaps ironic that only a gladiator's selection for and training in a *ludus* separated him from the criminals he was called on to slaughter in the arena. Although various criminals might be sentenced to the *ludi* and become gladiators, many of the more serious offenders were condemned instead to outright death in the arena, making them *noxii ad gladium ludi damnati*, or "condemned to be killed by the sword in the games." The *munerarius* took charge of these persons, guaranteeing that each would be killed within a year.

Usually at around noon, before the formal gladiatorial bouts had begun, guards herded the unarmed criminals onto the arena floor, where a group of fully armed gladiators quickly hacked some of them down. Others were crucified. And still others were tied to stakes, on which they were mangled and eaten by half-starved lions, bears, and other beasts. Often during these massacres, attendants veiled any emperors' statues adorning the amphitheater, symbolically sparing them the sight of "riffraff" in their death throes. Supposedly, the emperor Claudius, Caligula's successor, ordered so many such executions that he had a statue of Augustus removed so that it would not have to be constantly veiled.

In time, Roman audiences eagerly anticipated a rather gruesome piece of theater associated with these executions. During the Republic, a notorious brigand and murderer named Laureolus was condemned to a particularly cruel arena death. His punishment later became the subject of a mime (short dramatic skit) composed by the poet Gaius Valerius Catullus in

Executions often took place in Roman arenas. Usually, the condemned were killed by gladiators or wild beasts. But sometimes they were crucified or burned, as in this scene from the 1951 film version of Quo Vadis.

the first century B.C. Then, in about A.D. 30, actors began periodically staging re-creations of Laureolus's execution before crowds in various amphitheaters. Later still, these presentations became real, rather than staged. In the Colosseum, starting in Domitian's reign, at the play's climax a condemned criminal took the actor's place and suffered a real execution that was guaranteed to satisfy the most jaded of spectators. The unfortunate individual was nailed to a cross and then, while still alive and conscious, mutilated and eaten by a bear. Martial described this grisly event, telling how

Laureolus, hanging on no sham cross, gave his naked flesh to a Caledonian bear. His lacerated limbs lived on, dripping gore, and in all his body, body there was none [i.e., his body had lost its normal shape]. Finally he met with the punishment he deserved; the guilty wretch had plunged a sword into his father's throat or his master's, or in his madness had robbed a temple of its secret gold, or laid a cruel torch to Rome. The criminal had outdone the misdeeds of ancient story; in him, what had been a play became an execution.[52]

In this spectacular scene from the 1962 film Barabbas, *spectators watch prisoners reenact a battle from earlier Roman history.*

Panthers for the Amphitheater Hunts

The difficulty of capturing the large numbers of animals needed for the amphitheater hunts is partially revealed in the surviving correspondence of the great Roman orator Cicero when he served as governor of the province of Cilicia (in southern Asia Minor) from 51 to 50 B.C. In the summer of 51 B.C., Cicero's friend Marcus Caelius Rufus was staging some animal shows in Rome and began begging Cicero to send him some Cilician panthers for his upcoming games. The following part of one exchange between the two men is taken from Jo-Ann Shelton's *As the Romans Did*.

Caelius to Cicero:
"In almost all my letters to you I have written about the panthers. . . . [But] you have not sent me [any yet]. . . . I am greatly concerned about this now, because I think I will have to make all the arrangements myself. . . . So please, dear friend, take on this task. . . . As soon as the panthers have been caught, you have with you the men I sent over on financial business to feed them and arrange for shipping."

Cicero to Caelius:
"About the panthers! The matter is being handled with diligence and according to my orders by men who are skillful hunters. But there is a remarkable scarcity of panthers. And they tell me that the few panthers left are complaining bitterly that they are the only animals in my province for whom traps are set. . . . But the matter is receiving careful attention. . . . Any animal found will be yours."

Unfortunate substitutes for Laureolus continued to die in this same manner in the Colosseum and other amphitheaters across the Empire until at least A.D. 200.

Other Kinds of Arena Fights

Besides the gladiatorial bouts and public executions, the other common form of killing witnessed by the spectators at amphitheaters was the wild animal hunts, the *venationes*. Actually, the term *hunt* is a bit of a misnomer. Rather than sportsmen stalking wild creatures in their natural habitats, these shows featured the out-and-out slaughter of creatures who had no chance of escape, or fights between humans and beasts or between beasts and beasts. Throughout the second and well into the first century B.C., the *venationes* were minor spectacles presented mainly in the morning prior to the *munera* proper. The morning audience tended to be small, since this was when most Romans were busy working or attending to personal affairs. The hunts grew increasingly popular, however. And by the late Republic and early Empire, the larger-scale *venationes* were staged in the afternoon, drew big crowds, and sometimes lasted for several days.

Over the course of time, the number of animals butchered by the popular and famous Carpophorus and his fellow hunters must have been enormous. And of course, to this gruesome toll must be added that of animals killing other animals. According to Martial, some creatures were driven to fight in ways that they would have avoided in the wild:

A tigress that tended to lick the hand of the fearless trainer fiercely tore a wild lion with rabid tooth; a novelty, unknown in any times. She dared do no such thing while she lived in the high forests, but since she has been among us she has gained ferocity.[53]

A few sample numbers illustrate the huge scope of the carnage inflicted during the arena hunts. About 9,000 animals died during the 100 days of Titus's inauguration of the Colosseum in A.D. 80. And at least 11,000 were butchered in 107 when the emperor Trajan presented immense spectacles lasting 123 days. Later, in the lavish games given in 248 by the emperor Philip the "Arab" to celebrate the thousandth anniversary of Rome's founding, a partial list of the animals slaughtered included 32 elephants, 10 elk, 10 tigers, 70 lions, 30 leopards, 10 hyenas, 6 hippopotamuses, 1 rhinoceros, 10 giraffes, 20 wild asses, and 40 wild horses. In all, during the nearly five or six centuries in which such shows remained popular, millions of animals must have met their doom.

Another kind of amphitheater or arena fight involved hundreds, and occasionally thousands, of men manning full-sized ships that grappled in mock naval battles. These events, called *naumachiae*, were most often staged in basins and on lakes. The roles of sailors and soldiers in the rival fleets of such a staged sea battle were played by criminals and war captives, who customarily fought to the death. Often, the fighters were outfitted to represent the participants of famous historical naval battles; the Greek-Persian encounter at Salamis (in 480 B.C.) was especially popular and often repeated. Caesar staged a *naumachia* in 46 B.C. in a basin dug in the Campus Martius. Some one thousand sailors and two thousand oarsmen, dressed as rival Egyptians and Phoenicians, took part. And Augustus held one of the most impressive such shows on record in 2 B.C., later bragging,

I presented to the people an exhibition of a naval battle across the Tiber where a

A Testimonial to Titus's Naval Battle

In this excerpt from his *Epigrams*, Martial heaps lavish praise on the emperor Titus for staging a large sea fight in the same area (near the Tiber) previously used by Augustus for the same purpose. The frequent references to mythology, though now obscure, were perfectly clear to Martial's readers.

"It had been Augustus's labor to pit fleets against each other here and rouse the waters with naval clarion [noise]. How small a part is this our Caesar [Titus]! Thetis and Galatea [legendary sea nymphs] saw in the waves beasts they never knew. Triton [a merman and son of the sea god Neptune] saw chariots in hot career in the sea's dust [foam] and thought his master's [i.e., Neptune's] horses had passed by. As Nereus [a sea god known for his wisdom] prepared fierce battle for ferocious ships, he was startled to find himself walking on foot in the liquid expanse [possibly a reference to a floating platform on which gladiators fought]. Whatever is viewed in the Circus and the Amphitheater, that, Caesar, the wealth of your water has afforded you. So no more of Fucine [the lake in which Claudius staged his famous naval fight] and the lake of the direful Nero [who also put on a sea battle]; let this [i.e., Titus's version] be the only sea fight known to posterity."

This modern drawing shows a naval battle staged in an amphitheater. In reality, it is doubtful that such structures were flooded in this manner.

grove of the Caesars now is, having had the site excavated 1,800 feet in length and 1,200 feet in width. . . . Exclusive of rowers, there were about 3,000 combatants [who took part in the battle].[54]

The last *naumachia* mentioned in surviving ancient records was that presented by Philip the Arab at his millennial games in 248.

Presumably, the huge expense of these spectacles made any further attempts to stage them impractical. They turned out to be largely an extravagant novelty that was little missed once it was gone. However, the mainstays of the amphitheater games—gladiatorial bouts and wild beast shows—continued and remained widely popular for centuries to come.

CHAPTER 5

The Great Gladiator Rebellion of Spartacus

Modern authors who write about gladiators and their violent profession often make the point that, once these individuals had been captured, condemned, or otherwise recruited, they had no choice but to train and fight. They were watched and guarded day and night in their barracks and anywhere else their keepers allowed them to go. So, escape was all but impossible.

Indeed, in general, this bleak scenario was true throughout the long centuries in which the Romans maintained the gladiatorial institution, with one major exception. An unusual and dramatic series of events occurred in a roughly three-year period beginning in 73 B.C. A group of slaves at a *ludus* run by a *procurator* named Lentulus Batiatus near Capua, in Campania, broke out and began terrorizing the surrounding countryside. From the ranks of these escapees rose an unusually capable leader named Spartacus, under whose guidance the group freed many slaves in Italy. The gladiators trained a large number of the slaves to fight effectively and thereby created a formidable military force that managed to defeat several small Roman armies sent against it. The rebels created so much mayhem and fear that many Romans accorded the uprising the status of a full-fledged war, calling it the "War of Spartacus."

Despite the numerous victories achieved by the rebellious gladiators and their makeshift army, in the long run they had no chance against the full force of the Roman military,

the most formidable in the ancient world. Yet in a way, Spartacus and his followers did not die in vain. Over the centuries, they became a symbol of resistance to slavery and oppression and a model of raw courage and human dignity. Moreover, in the twentieth century the name Spartacus became a household word. In 1951 writer Howard Fast published an acclaimed and widely read novel about the great gladiator rebellion, and in 1960 producer Kirk Douglas and director Stanley Kubrick turned Fast's novel into a spectacular and moving film, with Douglas in the title role.

The novel and film are essentially faithful to historical truth. However, for the sake of dramatic effect, they condense, rearrange, or take other liberties with the events depicted in the ancient sources. The two principal ancient sources for the rebellion are Plutarch's biography of the Roman nobleman Marcus Licinius Crassus, who finally defeated Spartacus, and *The Civil Wars*, a work by Appian, a second-century-A.D. Romanized Greek scholar. A few other ancient writers, among them Sextus Julius Frontinus (first century A.D.) and Paulus Orosius (fifth century A.D.), made briefer mention of the gladiator revolt. By examining and carefully comparing these and other ancient accounts, modern scholars have been able to piece together a fairly reliable picture of how Spartacus and his fellow inmates escaped from their gladiator school and went on to terrorize large portions of Italy.

Spartacus's Story Becomes a Novel

In this excerpt from an interview for the AncientSites website, novelist Howard Fast tells how he came to write *Spartacus*, his famous book about the gladiator who led a rebellion against Rome.

"All my life I have always been intensely interested in the struggles of the poor and of working people against their oppressors. And the fact that Spartacus put together an army of slaves that almost destroyed Rome intrigued me. His name seemed to me symbolic of all the revolts of that kind through history. . . . [In 1950] I was imprisoned for contempt of Congress for refusing to 'name names' to the House Un-American Affairs Committee. This set me to thinking a great deal about prison, and when I was released, I began a very intense study of ancient slavery and imprisonment. . . . [The] books [I read contained] extensive information on the Spartacus revolt. . . . Then I set out to write the story of Spartacus. [It] was not an easy or simple book to write, but I got it written, and I felt that it was one of my best efforts. I sent it to my publisher . . . but acting on the advice of [FBI director] J. Edgar Hoover, they rejected it, as did seven other leading publishers. . . . So I decided to publish the book myself . . . sinking a lot of money into it. . . . I put it out in hardcover, and it sold 45,000 copies. In paperback, it has sold millions. . . . Then Kirk Douglas stepped into the picture and offered to do the film with Stanley Kubrick directing. Stanley and I became very close, and we worked on the film for months. . . . That was some forty years ago [and] 'Spartacus' is still being shown both in theatres and on television!"

In this shot from the film version of the story, the head trainer uses the body of Spartacus (Kirk Douglas) to illustrate the most effective spots for killing or wounding an opponent.

Escape from the Gladiator School

Though all the ancient sources agree that Spartacus was a gladiator, it is unknown whether he ever actually fought in the arena. The sources say only that he was confined in and escaped from a gladiator school, so it is possible that he was still a trainee at the time the rebellion started. The exact way he became a gladiator at the school is uncertain, and his personal background is sketchy. According to Plutarch, "He was a Thracian from the nomadic tribes [of Thrace]."[55] Appian adds that Spartacus "had once fought against the Romans and after being taken prisoner and sold had become a gladiator."[56] This scenario is highly probable, because in 74 and 73 B.C. the Romans were fighting a war against Mithridates, the ruler of a kingdom on the southern shore of the Black Sea, near Thrace; Spartacus probably fought in Mithridates' army until he was captured and shipped to Italy. As for Spartacus's personal attributes, Plutarch says that he

In another scene from Spartacus, *shortly before the escape, the gladiator trainees grimly filed by the body of one of their number who was executed for breaking the rules.*

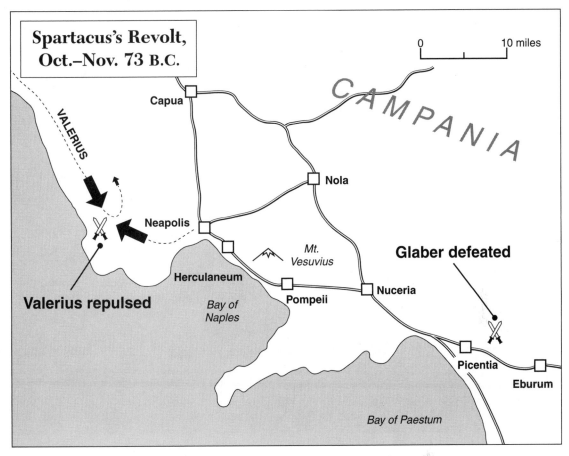

Spartacus's Revolt, Oct.–Nov. 73 B.C.

not only had a great spirit and great physical strength, but was, much more than one would expect from his condition [i.e., that he was a lowly slave and gladiator], most intelligent and cultured, being more like a Greek than a Thracian. . . . His wife . . . came from the same tribe and . . . shared in his escape and was then living with him.[57]

It is unlikely that an enemy soldier captured by the Romans and sold to a gladiator school would be allowed to take his wife with him. Spartacus probably met the woman Plutarch mentions in the school.

About the now famous escape from the school, Appian says only that the gladiators "overpowered their guards and escaped."[58] Plutarch provides a little more detail:

The rising of the gladiators and their devastation of Italy, which is generally known as the War of Spartacus, began as follows. A man called Lentulus Batiatus had an establishment for gladiators at Capua. Most of them were Gauls [from central Europe] and Thracians [from northern Greece]. They had done nothing wrong, but simply because of the cruelty of their owner were kept in close confinement until the time came for them to engage in combat. Two hundred of them planned to escape, but their plan was betrayed and only seventy-eight, who realized this,

Spartacus (holding a torch at center) celebrates with his troops after capturing the camp of C. Claudius Glaber, who had been sent to crush the rebels.

managed to act in time and get away, armed with choppers and spits which they seized from some cookhouse. On the road they came across some wagons which were carrying arms for gladiators to another city, and they took these arms for their own use.[59]

Spartacus's Early Victories

The first Roman force to attempt to recapture the escaped gladiators was the small garrison of soldiers stationed in nearby Capua. Sparta-cus and his companions easily defeated them, which prompted the government to send a larger force of three thousand soldiers under an officer named C. Claudius Glaber. While these troops were on their way, the gladiators took up a defensive position somewhere atop the cliffs along one side of Mt. Vesuvius, which loomed not far from Batiatus's school. Glaber blocked the only path leading up to the cliffs and, thinking he had his prey trapped, made camp and settled down for a siege. However, Spartacus outsmarted him. The cliffs were overgrown with vines, and the gladiators used these to climb down. They then sneaked around behind the Romans, launched a surprise attack (perhaps at night), sent Glaber and his men packing, and seized their camp.

In the months that followed, Spartacus began to build an unusual army, one made up only of slaves. "He allowed many domestic slaves and some free farm hands to join him," Appian states. Many Roman slaves had no fighting skills, but they now had the advantage of having professional warriors as teachers. Moreover, the larger the slave army grew, the bolder its members became. "With the gladiators Oenomaus and Crixus as his subordinates," Appian continues, Spartacus "plundered the nearby areas, and because he divided the spoils in equal shares his numbers quickly swelled."[60]

Soon the Roman government sent a second expedition against the gladiators, this one led by Publius Varinus. A number of skirmishes ensued between the opposing forces; unfortunately, little detail is known about these encounters. Both Plutarch and Appian say that Spartacus managed to capture Varinus's horse, a tremendous blow to Roman pride. Also, Frontinus mentions another example of the successful use of stealth and trickery by the gladiators. When Spartacus's camp was surrounded by the Romans, his men

> placed stakes at short intervals before the gate of the camp. Then, setting up corpses dressed in clothes and furnished with weapons, [they] tied these to the stakes to give the appearance of sentries when viewed from a distance. [They] also lighted fires throughout the whole camp. Deceiving the enemy by this empty show, Spartacus by night silently led out his troops.[61]

Fear Grips Rome

When word reached Rome that Varinus had been shamefully defeated, for the first time since the breakout from the gladiator school, Roman officials grew fearful. About a third of the population of Italy was composed of slaves. Most households had at least one or two slaves, and many had five to ten or more. Roman masters always dreaded the possibility that their human property might turn on them. Roman leaders now worried that if the gladiators and their army continued to score victories, a full-scale slave uprising might occur. As Plutarch puts it,

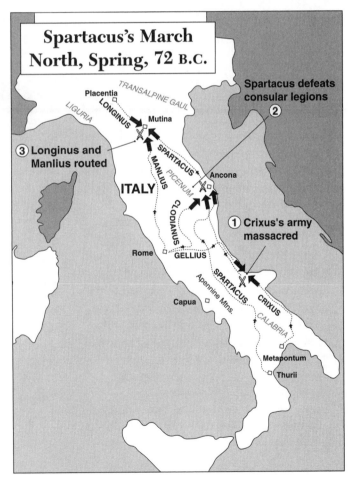

Spartacus's March North, Spring, 72 B.C.

There was now more to disturb the Senate than just the shame and disgrace of the revolt. The situation had become dangerous enough to inspire real fear, and as a result both consuls [the two administrator generals who served jointly as heads of state] were sent out to deal with what was considered a major war and a most difficult one to fight.[62]

One of the consuls, L. Gellius Publicola, scored an early victory. Spartacus's chief lieutenant, Crixus, had unwisely detached the German contingent of the gladiator/slave army and struck out on his own. Late in 72 B.C., near Mt. Garganus, in Apulia (in southeastern Italy), Gellius surprised and decisively defeated Crixus. However, Spartacus maneuvered the remainder of his army to meet the

The Man Who Defeated Spartacus

Marcus Licinius Crassus (ca. 115–53 B.C.), the Roman leader who put down the rebellion of gladiators and slaves, was a wealthy financier and politician. In addition to his defeat of Spartacus, he is best known as one of the members of the so-called First Triumvirate, the powerful political alliance that also included the famous military generals Julius Caesar and Gnaeus Pompeius ("Pompey"). The young Crassus served under the general and dictator Sulla, who rewarded him with estates confiscated from rich enemies. Crassus continued to amass wealth through silver mining and the slave trade. He used his wealth to bolster his political connections and influence and in 71 B.C. obtained command of an army to go after Spartacus.

Despite the success of the campaign, in the years that followed, Crassus felt himself overshadowed by Pompey's military brilliance and popularity, and the two became rivals. Caesar managed to get both men to reconcile long enough to form the Triumvirate in 60 B.C. But Crassus could not match the growing reputations of the other two men. Seeking more military glory of his own, he put all of his energies into a military campaign against the Parthian (Persian) Empire. In 53 B.C., at Carrhae (in Mesopotamia), Crassus was badly defeated and lost his life. Reportedly, Parthian officers cut off his head and right hand and presented them to their king.

A surviving bust of Spartacus's nemesis, the wealthy financier Marcus Licinius Crassus.

other consul, C. Lentulus Clodianus, and crushed the Roman force. The rebels also clashed with an army led by C. Cassius Longinus, governor of Cisalpine Gaul (the province encompassing the northernmost region of Italy). According to Plutarch, "Cassius was defeated and, after losing many of his men, only just managed to escape with his own life."[63]

Surprised and horrified at these Roman defeats, the Roman Senate appointed the wealthy and influential Crassus to put down the insurrection. "Because of his reputation or because of their friendship with him, large numbers of the nobility volunteered to serve with him,"[64] Plutarch writes. Unfortunately for Crassus, his campaign got off to an embarrassing start. He ordered one of his officers, a man named Mummius, to take a small force and follow Spartacus's army until Crassus himself had positioned his main army to strike. Mummius had direct orders not to engage the enemy; however, perhaps out of arrogant contempt for "mere slaves," Mummius ignored his orders, attacked, and suffered a resounding defeat.

Crassus Pursues the Rebels

The enraged Crassus now felt obliged to punish Mummius and a number of Romans who had thrown away their weapons in a mad dash to escape from the gladiators. This gave Spartacus time to move unopposed through Lucania (in southwestern Italy) to the sea. There, according to Plutarch,

> He fell in with some pirate ships from Cilicia [in what is now southern Turkey] and formed the plan of landing 2,000 men in Sicily and seizing the island; he would be able, he thought, to start another revolt of the slaves there, since the previous slave war [fought in Sicily from 104 to 100 B.C.]

had recently died down and only needed a little fuel to make it blaze out again.[65]

This audacious plan never materialized, mainly because the Cilician pirates betrayed Spartacus. After he had paid them large quantities of valuables he had amassed during his raids, they sailed away and left him without any ships.

Disappointed, Spartacus next established a base in the peninsula of Rhegium (the toe of the Italian "boot"). By this time, Crassus was in pursuit with his army and saw an opportunity to trap the gladiators and slaves in the peninsula. The Romans quickly built a ditch fifteen feet wide and some forty miles long, all backed up by a high earthen wall; this was intended to cut off the rebels' escape route back into Italy's heartland. However, the wily Spartacus waited until a storm blew up. That night, his troops filled in part of the ditch with tree branches and other debris. Most of the slave army crossed over this artificial bridge before Crassus could stop them.

At this point, Crassus may well have feared that his foe would march northward and attack Rome itself. After all, the possibility that hundreds of thousands more slaves might flee their masters and join the gladiators was only too real. A force that large might have a credible chance of seizing or laying waste to large portions of the capital city. Crassus also worried about the fact that the Senate had recently recalled one of Rome's greatest generals, Gnaeus Pompeius ("Pompey"), from a campaign in Spain to help crush the uprising. As Plutarch points out, Crassus knew "that the credit for the success would be likely to go not to himself but to the commander who appeared on the scene with reinforcements," so "he made all haste he could to finish the war" before Pompey arrived.[66]

Aiding Crassus in this enterprise was dissension in the ranks of the rebels. The ancient sources are a bit confusing regarding their exact

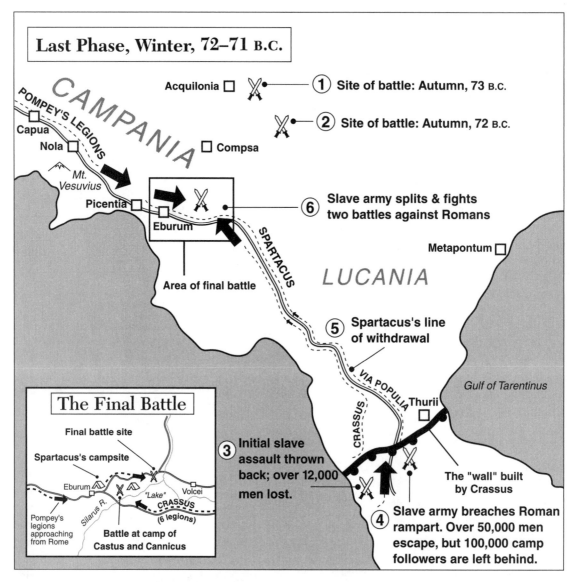

Last Phase, Winter, 72–71 B.C.

Acquilonia ☐ ⚔️ • —— ① Site of battle: Autumn, 73 B.C.

⚔️ • —— ② Site of battle: Autumn, 72 B.C.

POMPEY'S LEGIONS

CAMPANIA

Capua ☐
Nola ☐
☐ Compsa

Mt. Vesuvius

Picentia ☐
Eburum ☐ ⚔️ • —— ⑥ Slave army splits & fights two battles against Romans

SPARTACUS

Metapontum ☐

Area of final battle

LUCANIA

⑤ Spartacus's line of withdrawal

VIA POPULIA

Thurii

CRASSUS

Gulf of Tarentinus

The Final Battle

Final battle site

Spartacus's campsite

Eburum ☐ ⚔️ 🏔️ "Lake" Volcei ☐

Silarus R.   CRASSUS (6 legions)

Pompey's legions approaching from Rome

Battle at camp of Castus and Cannicus

③ Initial slave assault thrown back; over 12,000 men lost.

The "wall" built by Crassus

④ Slave army breaches Roman rampart. Over 50,000 men escape, but 100,000 camp followers are left behind.

motivations and moves, but it appears that a large force of Germans and Gauls led by the gladiators Castus and Cannicus separated from the main body of Spartacus's army and struck out on their own. Frontinus gives the most reliable account of Crassus's assault on this splinter group in Lucania:

> Crassus fortified two camps close beside the camp of the enemy, near Mt. Can-

tenna. Then, one night, he moved his forces, leading them all out and positing them at the base of the mountain . . . leaving his headquarters tent in the larger camp in order to deceive the enemy.[67]

Under cover of darkness, Crassus divided his troops into two groups. One contingent threatened (but probably did not directly attack) Spartacus, thereby keeping the main rebel force busy. Meanwhile, Crassus moved with his main force against Castus and Cannicus. Pretending to flee from the gladiators, the Romans led the enemy into a trap. "When the barbarians followed," Frontinus says,

the [Roman] cavalry fell back to the flanks [sides], and suddenly the Roman [infantry] force disclosed [revealed] itself and rushed forward with a shout. In that battle . . . thirty-five thousand armed men [of the slave army], with their commanders, were slain. [68]

The Final Battle

Though Crassus's victory was a major setback for the rebels, Spartacus soon followed up with another victory of his own, routing two of

An eighteenth-century engraving captures the dramatic moment when Spartacus slew his horse, saying that if he won the battle he could get plenty of horses from the defeated Romans.

Crassus's officers in a small pitched battle. However, this win actually turned out to be the gladiators' undoing. Large numbers of the rebels grew overconfident, seeming to believe that they could now easily finish Crassus off and thereafter have free rein to do as they pleased. Against the wishes of Spartacus and his leading officers, the army marched on and confronted Crassus; Spartacus evidently felt he had no choice but to do whatever he could to help his followers achieve victory.

The final battle took place late in 71 B.C. near the Silarus River in northern Lucania. Although few details have survived, the gladiators and slaves seem to have fought courageously before they were overwhelmed. As for Spartacus himself, Plutarch writes,

When his horse was brought to him, he drew his sword and killed it, saying that the enemy had plenty of good horses which would be his if he won, and, if he lost, he would not need a horse at all. Then he made straight for Crassus himself, charging forward through the press of weapons and wounded men, and, though he did not reach Crassus, he cut down two centurions [unit leaders] who fell on [attacked] him together. Finally, when his own men had taken to flight, he himself, surrounded by enemies, still stood his ground and died fighting to the last.[69]

Appian gives a slightly different version, saying that Spartacus "was wounded by a spear-

In the final battle, as staged for Kubrick's film, the army of gladiators and slaves (in the foreground) faces the formal battle array of the Roman legions.

Punishment for Those Who Fled

In this excerpt from his *Life of Crassus* (in *Fall of the Roman Republic*), Plutarch tells how Crassus punished the soldiers who had dropped their weapons and fled from Spartacus and the gladiators.

"Crassus . . . re-armed his soldiers and made them give guarantees that in the future they would preserve the arms in their possession. Then he took 500 of those who had been the first to fly [from the battlefield] and had shown themselves the greatest cowards, and, dividing them into fifty squads of ten men each, put to death one man, chosen by lot, from each squad. This was a traditional method of punishing soldiers, now revived by Crassus after having been out of use for many years. Those who are punished in this way not only lose their lives, but are also disgraced, since the whole army are there as spectators, and the actual circumstances of the execution are very savage and repulsive."

thrust in the thigh, but went down on one knee, held his shield in front of him, and fought off his attackers until he and a great number of his followers were encircled and fell."[70]

The number of Spartacus's followers killed in the battle and mop-up operations is unknown, but it may have been as high as fifty to sixty thousand. Crassus lost no more than a thousand men. Afterward, the six thousand surviving rebels suffered crucifixion along the road to Rome as a warning to others who might contemplate threatening the established order. (In the film, Spartacus survives the battle and is among those crucified; he lives long enough to see his wife and infant son escape to freedom, an unhistoric but dramatically moving touch.) After the War of Spartacus, Rome had no more major gladiatorial or slave rebellions, but the authorities remained ever fearful and vigilant and made sure that the gladiator schools were secure.

Social and Moral Aspects of Amphitheater Fights

The public images of gladiators and other arena fighters, as well as the way they were treated outside the arena, reflected the Romans' own unique cultural and social values. Roman society was clearly fascinated by and highly preoccupied with gladiators and the amphitheater games. Yet the relationship between society and arena fighters was not one of love but, rather, of love-hate.

A Bad Reputation

Indeed, when it came to gladiators, most Romans were caught up in an obsessive and seemingly contradictory form of hero worship. On the one hand, socially speaking these warriors were viewed as debased, worthless, and undignified low-life, and like actors and other entertainers, gladiators bore the degrading stigma of *infamia* ("bad reputation"). The second-century-B.C. Latin writer Calpurnius Flaccus put it bluntly: "There is no meaner condition among the people than that of the gladiator."[71]

The low social standing of gladiators and other arena fighters had a strong negative effect on their lives, affecting their public image, self-esteem, social opportunities, and much more. People commonly referred to them as crude (*importunus*), indecent (*obscaenus*), damned (*damnatus*), and hopeless (*perditus*). And writers routinely slandered or poked fun at them, often comparing them directly or indirectly to prostitutes, criminals, effeminate actors, and other characters widely seen as unsavory. Because a majority of gladiators began as slaves or

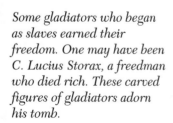
Some gladiators who began as slaves earned their freedom. One may have been C. Lucius Storax, a freedman who died rich. These carved figures of gladiators adorn his tomb.

Though Roman society labeled gladiators low-life characters, their macho image appealed to many. The emperor Caligula, seen here, is said to have enjoyed the company of gladiators.

prisoners, large numbers of them were bought and sold like cattle. Even those who gained their freedom (or were free when they became gladiators) were widely seen as no better than slaves.

Even in death, many gladiators could not escape their degrading social status. Society denied an arena fighter proper burial; this was possible only if a relative, friend, or admirer claimed the body and buried it privately. Among the evidence for this sad state of affairs is an inscription found at the site of ancient Sarsina (in northeastern Italy). The inscription states that three classes of people are not allowed in the town's new cemetery: suicides by hanging, those involved in immoral trades (i.e., prostitutes, actors, and so on), and gladiators.

At the same time, however, all of this public scorn for and social discrimination against gladiators was contradicted by the fact that their exploits in the arena were often admired. And those arena fighters who won many bouts often became heroes no less popular than today's biggest football, baseball, and basketball stars. These fortunate few usually won their freedom (if they began as slaves); enjoyed the applause and sometimes the gifts of fans (including large sums of money and estates given by emperors to a selected few); and could have their pick of beautiful young women (who were the equivalent of the groupies who sometimes attach themselves to modern rock stars). In one of his epigrams, Martial heaps praise on one such arena hero. "Hermes, favorite fighter of the age," it begins.

> Hermes, skilled in all weaponry; Hermes, gladiator and trainer both; Hermes, tempest [storm] and tremor [earthquake] of his school . . . Hermes, taught to win without wounding [i.e., by disarming his opponents] . . . Hermes, darling and distress

of gladiators' women [i.e., they either loved him or feared he would kill their men] . . . Hermes, glory of Mars [god of war] universal; Hermes, all things in one and thrice unique. [72]

The Virtue of Submission

It is only natural to wonder what was behind this tremendous outpouring of adulation for arena fighters. The reasons appear to have been closely related to the Romans' peculiar and conservative ethical notions about the nature of honor and the virtue of submission to authority. For instance, because a gladiator offered up his own blood to please others, society saw him as a sadly tragic but still heroic figure to be admired and honored. The gladiator had taken a solemn oath that he (or she) would die, unflinchingly and unhesitatingly, for an audience of "betters." Such an act of complete and ultimate submission to the will of one's "master" made the gladiator, in Roman eyes, a model for a person of honor. In a powerfully worded passage, Cicero wrote,

Consider the blows they [gladiators] endure! Consider how they who have been well-disciplined prefer to accept a blow than shamefully avoid it! How often it is made clear that they consider nothing other than the satisfaction of their master or the people! Even when they are covered with wounds they send a messenger to their master to inquire his will. If they have given satisfaction to their masters, they are pleased to fall. What even mediocre gladiator ever groans, ever alters the expression on his face? Which one of them acts shamefully either standing or falling? And which of them, even when he does suc-

cumb, ever contracts his neck when ordered to receive the [death] blow? [73]

Cicero tried to put into words one of the more basic cultural beliefs of Roman society, namely that submission to higher authority was part of the natural order and therefore a good thing. This belief was one of the pillars supporting the Roman political and patronage systems, which relied on many dependent persons (clients) submitting to and doing the bidding of a few "superiors" (patrons). The belief was also deeply imbedded in popular religion; the gods represented an authority that even the mightiest human was obliged to submit to and obey.

Thus, when a gladiator bravely faced and accepted death, he was for an instant transformed into a version of one of Rome's most ideal figures—the soldier who gives his life for the homeland. And in that brief, sublime moment, he and his audience connected with, ennobled, and empowered each other. The always insightful Seneca offered the following military analogy comparing a gladiator to a soldier called on by his general (and the state) to shed blood and die if necessary:

Soldiers glory in their wounds and gladly vaunt themselves over the blood they were privileged to shed; though those who returned from the fray unhurt may have fought as well, the man who brings back a wound is more respected. . . . The recruit pales at the thought of a wound; the veteran can look at his flowing gash with composure, for he knows that he has often won the victory after losing blood. . . . So God hardens and scrutinizes and exercises those he approves and loves. . . . The most hazardous duties are assigned to the bravest soldiers. . . . And no man in such a detachment will say, "The general has treated me badly," but rather, "The general thinks well of me." Similarly, those told to undergo what cowards and weaklings would weep over should say, "God has judged us fit subjects to test how much human nature can endure."[74]

This military analogy, in which gladiators and their combats are compared favorably and honorably to the lives and exploits of Roman soldiers, gained further strength from widespread interest in legendary battles and warriors of the dim past. Both the Romans and Greeks had a fond nostalgia for the "good old days" (often referred to as the "Age of Heroes"), when the most formidable warriors supposedly faced off in one-on-one duels before their assembled armies, as in Homer's *Iliad.* In a very real way, gladiators' arena exploits recalled the courage and honor of such ancient combats.

A gladiator was expected to die unflinchingly and with honor to satisfy an audience of "betters." Here, a defeated fighter waits calmly while his opponent looks for the signal to kill or spare him.

A Superstitious Awe of Death?

Whatever the reasons for Rome's strange contradictory views about gladiators and other arena fighters, most people simply accepted and perpetuated them without thinking. A few, however, viewed them as disquieting, even unethical and twisted. The Christian apologist Tertullian was one who had the courage to commit his concerns about it to paper. "Men give them [gladiators] their souls, women their bodies too," he stated with unconcealed disdain.

> On one and the same account, they glorify them and degrade and diminish them—indeed, they openly condemn them to ignominy [dishonor and humiliation] and the loss of civil rights, excluding them from the Senate House and rostrum [speaker's platform], the senatorial and equestrian [social] orders, and all other honors or distinctions of any type. The perversity of it! Yet, they love whom they punish; they belittle whom they esteem; the art they glorify, the artist they debase. What judgment is this? On account of that for which he is vilified [condemned], he [the gladiator] is deemed worthy of merit![75]

Lurking beneath this societal judgment that so irked Tertullian, especially the unabashed fascination that millions of Romans had with watching gladiators kill one another, was an added psychological aspect. The appeal of the bloody arena may have constituted the outward expression of something unhealthy that was deeply ingrained in Roman culture—a superstitious awe of and interest in death. It is possible that death scenes described in literature or acted out on the stage were not enough to satisfy the gnawing desire to decipher the mysteries surrounding death, in a sense to dissect and examine death and thereby understand it. Moreover, in the minds of many Romans, nothing could substitute for being close to and studying the real thing.

For instance, Seneca described a favorite leisure pursuit at upper-class banquets—placing mullet fish in empty glass containers and watch-

---

A Senator's Wife Shames Herself

Not only did society see gladiators as disreputable, wretched characters, it equally condemned ordinary people who entered into intimate relationships with them. In his sixth satire, Juvenal unleashes his witty wrath on Eppia, an upper-class woman who fell in love with and ran off with a gladiator.

"That senator's wife, Eppia, eloped with her fancy swordsman. . . . Husband, family, sister, all were jettisoned [abandoned], [with] not one single thought for her country; shamelessly she forsook her tearful children. . . . What was the youthful charm that so fired our senator's wife? What hooked her? What did Eppia see in him to make her put up with being labeled 'The Gladiatress'? Her darling, her Sergius, was no chicken [youngster], [but was] forty at least, with a dud arm that held promise of [his] early retirement. Besides, his face looked like a proper mess, helmet-scarred, a great zit on his nose, [and] an unpleasant discharge from one constantly weeping eye. What of it? *He was a gladiator*. . . . This is what she preferred to her children and her country."

Gladiatorial bouts, such as this clash between a retiarius *and a* myrmillo, *were in a sense rituals of death, with which Roman society had a deep fascination.*

ing the change of colors produced by their death throes. "There is nothing, you say, more beautiful than a dying mullet," Seneca wrote in his treatise *Natural Questions*. "In the very struggle of its failing breath of life, first a red, then a pale tint suffuses it, and its scales change hue, and between life and death there is a gradation into subtle shades."[76] The life-and-death struggles of the arena may well have constituted a human version of this peculiar custom, both versions having been shaped by a deep-seated and compelling awe of death.

Considering these and other ingrained cultural concepts, it would be too easy, as well as misguided, to view the Roman captivation with gladiators simply as an expression of public depravity and sadism, which has often been suggested. Instead, the truth is far more complex.

During the amphitheater shows, both the performers and the spectators took part in ceremonies and rituals that were part of deeply rooted social, religious, and ethical traditions and beliefs. The crowds who cheered as men and beasts died before their eyes were attracted and thrilled as much by the honorable and heroic display of courage in the face of death as by the excitement of the danger and spectacle of the slaughter. And what was on one level a form of entertainment was, beneath the surface, a ritualistic public expression of some of the most powerful core beliefs and values of both the individual and society.

"It Was Pure Murder"

These ingrained values can also be seen at work in the way most Romans automatically accepted the public executions regularly performed in the amphitheaters. The gruesome manner of these executions, as well as the fact that crowds watched and laughed as they occurred, seems extreme and disturbing to most people today. However, it must be remembered that the average Roman took the concept of capital punishment completely for granted. He or she also saw public humiliation as a fitting penalty for many crimes and maybe also as a deterrent to crime in general. For most of those who attended the amphitheater games, therefore, murderers and other heinous criminals who suffered public execution in the arena were simply receiving their just rewards.

On the other hand, at least a few Romans viewed such killings (and maybe gladiatorial fights and other kinds of arena bloodletting as well) as distasteful. Exactly how many and what types of people felt this way remains unclear. Excluding the Christians, whose numbers were for a long time very small, they may

The great orator Cicero was among the Roman intellectuals who were critical of the bloodier games.

have been primarily better-educated members of society, although this is no more than an assumption based on the fact that most of the surviving evidence consists of the testimony of upper-class intellectuals like Cicero and Seneca. Seneca disliked at least some aspects of the killing that went on in amphitheaters. That much is clear from a passage he penned after witnessing the execution of a group of unarmed condemned men:

> I happened on the noon interlude at the arena, expecting some clever burlesque, some relaxation to give the spectators a respite [break] from human gore. [But] the show was the reverse. The fighting that had gone before [i.e., the regular gladiatorial fights] was charity by contrast. Now there was no nonsense about it; it was pure

murder. The men have nothing to protect them; the whole body is exposed and every stroke tells. Many spectators prefer this to the usual matches. Why shouldn't they? There is no helmet or shield to parry the steel. Why armor? Why skill? Such things [merely] delay the [inevitable] kill.[77]

Seneca seemed to have a certain amount of sympathy for the arena fighters as well, or at least it was a sympathy for the "noble savage" trapped in servile conditions and forced to kill others, a situation that Seneca found distasteful and sad. He was therefore filled with admiration for those occasional arena fighters who defied the system and took their own lives rather than kill others on command. In a letter to a friend, Seneca describes two men—one from a beast show, the other from a *naumachia*—who, in his words, "insulted death" and chose their own fate:

Do not imagine that only great men have had the toughness to break through the trammels of human bondage. . . . Men of the meanest condition have made a mighty effort to break through to deliverance . . . and by their own strength transformed implements naturally harmless into weapons. Lately a German in the beast-fighting barracks who was practicing for the morning show excused himself to relieve his bowels— the only function for which the guards would allow him privacy. Then he took the sponge-tipped stick [used to clean the latrines] and rammed it down his throat and choked his breath till he suffocated. That was a way to insult death! . . . Stout fellow, the right man to let choose his own fate! . . . On this all will agree: the dirtiest death is preferable to the daintiest slavery. . . . I promised you more examples from the same exhibitions. In the second event of a

sea-fight spectacle one of the barbarians sank the whole spear which he was to use against his opponents down his own throat. "Why," he cried, "have I not long ago escaped all this torment, all this mockery?" . . . The show was the better worth looking at in the degree that men [and women who witnessed the act] learned that it is more decent to die than to kill.[78]

The Elephants' Revenge

Seneca was not the only upper-class Roman to express negative views about various aspects of the amphitheater shows. The second-century-A.D. emperor Marcus Aurelius, for example, thoroughly disliked the bloodletting that went on in the arena. He attended games at the Colosseum strictly out of a sense of duty to his subjects and often ignored the fighting, choosing to use the time for more constructive purposes such as dictating letters and conducting other state business.

In addition, a number of other Romans felt that the butchery of the arena was either vulgar and beneath their "refined" tastes or just plain boring. Evidently, Cicero and some of his friends fell into this group. In a letter written in 55 B.C., Cicero congratulated his friend Marcus Marius for not attending a violent spectacle. Cicero did attend the show, but only out of feelings of obligation to the man who staged it (the military general Gnaeus Pompeius), and afterward told Marius:

If it was some physical ailment or ill health which kept you from attending the spectacles, I would attribute your absence more to your luck than to your wisdom. But if you decided to scorn what other men marvel at, and chose not to attend, although

In this excerpt from his *Natural History* (John Healy's translation), Pliny the Elder describes the crowd's reactions to the mistreatment of the elephants in the games sponsored by Pompey in 55 B.C.

"One elephant put up a fantastic fight and, although its feet were badly wounded, crawled on its knees against the attacking bands [of hunters]. It snatched away their shields and hurled them into the air. . . . There was also an extraordinary incident with a second elephant when it was killed by a single blow: a javelin struck under its eye and penetrated the vital parts of its head. All the elephants *en masse* [in a group], tried to break out through the iron railings that enclosed them, much to the discomfiture of the spectators. . . . But when Pompey's elephants had given up hope of escape, they played on the sympathy of the crowd, entreating [pleading with] them with indescribable gestures. They moaned, as if wailing, and caused the spectators such distress that, forgetting Pompey and his lavish display . . . they rose in a body, in tears, and heaped dire curses on Pompey."

good health would have allowed you to, then I have two reasons to be delighted: first, because you were free from physical pain and, second, because your mind was strong, since you ignored things other men marvel at for no reason. . . . All and all, the entertainments were (if you're interested) quite splendid, but certainly not to your taste. . . . The spectacle of such extravagant expense destroyed any spontaneous merriment. . . . Things which won the applause of the common people would have given you no enjoyment. . . . I know that you certainly didn't worry about missing the athletes, since you have always been scornful of gladiators.[79]

Cicero himself was less bothered by the plight of the human fighters and more by that of the animals that suffered in the bloody *venationes,* seeing the slaughter of helpless beasts as both pitiful and disturbing. In the same letter to Marius, he expressed his misgivings after watching some six hundred lions and a number of elephants meet horrible deaths. Apparently, the plight of the ele-

phants bothered many others in the audience as well, which shows that there was a limit even to the high tolerance most Romans had for the violence of the arena. "There were wild animal hunts," Cicero continues,

two a day for five days, very expensive ones—no one can deny that. But what pleasure can a civilized man find when either a helpless human being is mangled by a very strong animal, or a magnificent animal is stabbed again and again with a hunting spear? Even if this was something to look at, you have seen it often enough before, and I, who was a spectator there, saw nothing new. The last day was the day for elephants. The mob of spectators was greatly impressed, but showed no real enjoyment. In fact, a certain sympathy arose for the elephants, and a feeling that there was a kind of affinity between that large animal and the human race.[80]

This moving account was corroborated by the noted Roman scholar Pliny the Elder, who later wrote about the same show, providing more detail, some of it heartrending, about the inhumane treatment of the elephants. He also recorded for posterity the undaunted courage shown by one of the doomed beasts. "One elephant put up a fantastic fight," he says, "and although its feet were badly wounded, [it] crawled on its knees against the attacking bands [of hunters]. It snatched away their shields and hurled them into the air."[81]

Interestingly, those Romans who felt that the mistreatment of the elephants that day had crossed a line also believed that there had to be some sort of retribution, either divine or natural, for the offense. After the pitiless slaughter of the elephants at Pompey's games, a rumor spread far and wide that when he had first captured the beasts, he had made them a promise. Namely, once they had entertained the humans, they would be allowed to return to their homeland unhurt. According to this scenario, Pompey betrayed the beasts by slaughtering them; his own untimely and gruesome murder a few years later was seen by some as the fulfillment of the elephants' revenge.

Arena hunters spar with wild beasts in this terra-cotta relief now on display in Rome. At least some Romans felt a measure of pity for the animals who were slaughtered.

Few or No Moral Objections

This notorious incident with the elephants aside, one must be careful not to read too much into these statements of sympathy, pity, and indignation by Seneca and Cicero. They and others who wrote similar tracts that have survived were highly educated, wealthy, and privileged, as well as being more concerned with ethical and moral behavior than the average person. They were far from being typical Romans, therefore. And for centuries to come, most of their countrymen had few or no objections— moral, intellectual, or otherwise—to gladiators killing either one another or condemned criminals, even if there was some occasional sympathy for courageous elephants. Only much later (in the mid–fourth century), when the Christians came to wield considerable political power in Rome, did such objections begin to become widespread. Eventually, the objectors would manage to eradicate altogether the time-honored *munera* and the gladiator schools that supplied them.

The Decline of the Gladiator

The bloody gladiatorial combats that had drawn Roman audiences into the amphitheaters for centuries might well have continued to flourish up to and even beyond A.D. 476, the year when the last Roman emperor in the western part of the realm was deposed. And in the eastern part, centered at Constantinople, the *munera* might have lasted until 1453, when the Turks captured that city, eclipsing the last remaining remnants of what had been the Roman Empire. However, these scenarios never happened. Instead, a momentous event occurred in the fourth century, one that was destined to bring the reign of the gladiator on Rome's public stage to an end. This event was the amazingly swift rise and political triumph of Christianity.

Christians are tied to stakes (at far right) in an early persecution. Eventually, after taking control of Rome's government, the Christians banned gladiatorial fights.

No one could have predicted that the Christians would gain control of the government and ban gladiators from the amphitheaters. The Christians had started out in the first century as a despised minority and in the years that followed had suffered in a number of persecutions instigated or encouraged by the state. Despite these problems, however, the faith persisted and slowly grew in popularity.

Then, in the early fourth century, the Christians' fortunes began to improve dramatically. First, in 313 the emperor Constantine issued an edict granting them religious freedom, and twenty-four years later he converted to Christianity on his deathbed. Constantine's steadfast support of the faith allowed it to gain acceptance and grow at a phenomenal rate; thereafter, all but one of Rome's emperors were Christians. [82]

As the Christians gained more and more power and influence in Roman society, they increasingly condemned the *munera*. They had long viewed the gladiatorial combats as both murder and an offense against humanity, often citing the Christian spokesman Tertullian. More than a century earlier, Tertullian had harshly denounced the gladiator's art, calling it murder. Fourth-century Christians now gave a new and strident voice to this view. It did not matter that a large proportion of Romans were still pagans (non-Christians), most of whom wanted the gladiatorial games to continue. They eventually had no choice but to give in to the increasing political power of the Christians, who finally came to control the government. At the urgings of Christian bishops like Ambrose, the emperor Theodosius I (died 395) banned the worship of the old Roman gods in favor of the Christian god. And by the end of the century, the gladiator schools had been closed. Gladiatorial fights still took place in the Colosseum from time to time for a few more years. But

Public Executions of Christians

Some early Christians were likely among those who were condemned to public execution in the Roman Colosseum. According to tradition, the first Christian who died in the great amphitheater was Saint Ignatius, bishop of Antioch, the first writer to refer to the church as "catholic," or universal. Supposedly, he welcomed martyrdom in the arena and exclaimed shortly before his death, "I am as the grain of the field, and must be ground by the teeth of the lions, that I may become fit for His [God's] table."

It is important to note, however, that the popular notion that the Romans were religiously intolerant and persecuted the Christians for having different beliefs is mistaken. The Romans were highly tolerant of others' beliefs and themselves practiced numerous alternative and often exotic religions from around the Mediterranean world. What made the early Christians different was that they condemned all other beliefs but their own and often refused to acknowledge the emperor's divinity. Moreover, they kept to themselves, appearing to be antisocial. So, over time, they acquired the stigma of having *odium generis humani*, a "hatred for the human race." Worst of all, unfounded rumors were spread that Christian rituals included cannibalism, incest, and other repugnant acts. Most Romans came to believe these rumors and therefore felt little or no pity for any of the Christians who may have met their deaths on the arena's blood-soaked sands.

The remains of the Colosseum, in Rome, where thousands of gladiators met their doom over the centuries. By the mid-500s B.C., the great amphitheater had permanently closed down.

by 430 at the latest, these combats had ceased forever.

The End of Self-Indulgence

Although gladiators no longer fought in the Colosseum and other amphitheaters, these facilities still presented spectacles to packed houses for more than another century. The animal hunts and public executions of criminals continued to be held, since Christian leaders apparently did not disapprove of them. Some surviving writings reveal that as late as 523, half a century after the last Roman emperor had been driven from his throne, the Colosseum still drew huge crowds to watch animal hunts. In addition, wrestling matches had become popular attractions, perhaps as nonlethal substitutes for the banned gladiatorial bouts. These games were well attended because Rome was still a large and vital city. And for a while, much of Italy remained prosperous under a capable Germanic leader, Theodoric the Ostrogoth.

However, not long after Theodoric's demise in 526, the city of Rome rapidly declined. Lacking the administration and services that the Roman government and, to a much lesser degree, Theodoric had provided, it increasingly fell into disrepair, and its population rapidly dwindled to a fraction of what it had been in its heyday. The large and complex governmental apparatus needed to pay for and stage the spectacles, as well as to maintain the huge facilities that housed them, was gone. And large crowds with the leisure time and enthusiasm to attend such games no longer existed in Rome or most other cities.

By the end of the sixth century, grass had begun to grow on the bleachers of the Colosseum and other amphitheaters, where for so long audiences had loudly cheered the arena warriors and with a turn of their thumbs decreed life or death. Long before, the far-sighted Seneca, who had made known his feelings about these fighters and their violent ways, had also foretold the end of the self-indulgent society that had spawned and supported them. "All the cities that have ever held dominion or have been the splendid jewels of empires," he wrote, "will be swept away. . . . Some will be ruined by wars, others will be destroyed by idleness and a peace that ends in sloth, or by luxury, the bane of those with great wealth."[83]

Notes

Introduction: Gladiators: Artifacts of a Different Worldview

1. Quoted in Jo-Ann Shelton, ed., *As the Romans Did: A Sourcebook in Roman Social History.* New York: Oxford University Press, 1988, p. 344.
2. Seneca, *Letters,* in Moses Hadas, trans. and ed., *The Stoic Philosophy of Seneca.* New York: W.W. Norton, 1958, p. 172.
3. Tertullian, *Apology,* quoted in Michael Grant, *Gladiators.* New York: Delacorte Press, 1967, p. 120.
4. Eckart Kohne, "Bread and Circuses: The Politics of Entertainment," in *Gladiators and Caesars: The Power of Spectacle in Ancient Rome,* ed. Eckart Kohne. Berkeley and Los Angeles: University of California Press, 2000, p. 12.
5. Alan Baker, *The Gladiator: The Secret History of Rome's Warrior Slaves.* New York: St. Martin's Press, 2000, pp. 3–4.
6. Stephen Wisdom, *Gladiators: 100 B.C.– A.D. 200.* Oxford, England: Osprey, 2001, p. 6.

Chapter 1: The Origins of Roman Gladiators

7. Quoted in Roland Auguet, *Cruelty and Civilization: The Roman Games.* London: Routledge, 1994, p. 21.
8. Homer, *Iliad,* trans. W.H.D. Rouse. New York: New American Library, 1950, p. 269.
9. Kohne, "Bread and Circuses," p. 11.
10. Livy, *The History of Rome from Its Foundation,* excerpted in *Livy,* vol. 2, trans. Canon Roberts. New York: E.P. Dutton, 1912, p. 125.
11. Livy, *History of Rome,* excerpted in *Livy: The War with Hannibal,* trans. Aubrey de Sélincourt. New York: Penguin, 1972, p. 205.
12. Vitruvius, *On Architecture,* trans. Frank Granger, 2 vols. Cambridge, Mass.: Harvard University Press, 1962, vol. 1, p. 255.
13. Baker, *The Gladiator,* pp. 11–12.
14. Prologue to Terence, *The Mother-in-Law,* in *Terence: The Comedies,* trans. Betty Radice. New York: Penguin, 1976, pp. 293–94.
15. See Plutarch, *Life of Caesar,* in *Fall of the Roman Republic: Six Lives by Plutarch,* trans. Rex Warner. New York: Penguin, 1972, p. 248.
16. Suetonius, *Julius Caesar,* in *Lives of the Twelve Caesars,* published as *The Twelve Caesars,* trans. Robert Graves, Rev. Michael Grant. New York: Penguin, 1979, p. 17.
17. Juvenal, *Satires,* published as *Juvenal: The Sixteen Satires,* trans. Peter Green. New York: Penguin, 1974, p. 207.
18. Quoted in Shelton, *As the Romans Did,* p. 336.
19. Alan Cameron, *Circus Factions: Blues and Greens at Rome and Byzantium.* London: Clarendon Press, 1976, pp. 173–74.

Chapter 2: Recruitment, Training, and Discipline

20. Quoted in Shelton, *As the Romans Did,* p. 345. Such volunteers, though theoretically still free during their tenures as gladiators, nevertheless temporarily had to endure both a reduction in status, to that of a slave, and the rigors of what was essentially a convict's life.
21. Grant, *Gladiators,* p. 31.
22. Baker, *The Gladiator,* p. 48.
23. Petronius, *The Satyricon,* trans. J.P. Sullivan. New York: Penguin, 1977, p. 128.

24. Auguet, *Cruelty and Civilization*, p. 158.
25. Pliny the Elder, *Pliny the Elder: Natural History: A Selection*, trans. John H. Healy. New York: Penguin, 1991, p. 159.
26. Kathleen Coleman, "The Virtues of Violence: Gladiators, the Arena, and the Roman System of Values," (lecture delivered at the College of the Holy Cross, Worcester, Mass., March 2001).
27. Graham Ashford, "The Classic Stance," *Ludus Gladiatorius*, 2002, pp. 3–4. www.ludus.org.uk.
28. Ashford, "Classic Stance," p. 4.
29. Ashford, "Classic Stance," p. 4.
30. Grant, *Gladiators*, pp. 49–50.
31. Coleman, "The Virtues of Violence."

Chapter 3: Many and Diverse Types of Arena Fighters

32. Auguet, *Cruelty and Civilization*, pp. 76–77.
33. Suetonius, *Caligula*, in *Twelve Caesars*, p. 171.
34. Wisdom, *Gladiators*, pp. 31–32.
35. Quoted in Grant, *Gladiators*, p. 61.
36. Quoted in Auguet, *Cruelty and Civilization*, p. 80.
37. Graham Ashford, "Dimachaerius," *Ludus Gladiatorius*, 2002, p. 1. www.ludus.org.uk.
38. Petronius, *Satyricon*, p. 59.
39. Auguet, *Cruelty and Civilization*, pp. 59–60.
40. Suetonius, *Caligula*, in *Twelve Caesars*, p. 169.
41. Suetonius, *Tiberius*, in *Twelve Caesars*, p. 117.
42. Juvenal, *Satires*, p. 136.
43. Tacitus, *The Annals*, published as *The Annals of Ancient Rome*, trans. Michael Grant. New York: Penguin, 1989, p. 360.
44. Martial, *Epigrams*, ed. and trans. D.R. Shackleton Bailey, 3 vols. Cambridge, Mass.: Harvard University Press, 1993, vol. 1, p. 25.

45. Richard C. Beacham, *Spectacle Entertainments of Early Imperial Rome*. New Haven, Conn.: Yale University Press, 1999, p. 12.

Chapter 4: Death in the Arena: Gladiators in Action

46. Auguet, *Cruelty and Civilization*, p. 44.
47. Auguet, *Cruelty and Civilization*, p. 56.
48. Auguet, *Cruelty and Civilization*, pp. 57–58.
49. Martial, *Epigrams*, vol. 1, pp. 33–35.
50. Petronius, *Satyricon*, pp. 59–60.
51. Quoted in Auguet, *Cruelty and Civilization*, p. 53.
52. Martial, *Epigrams*, vol. 1, p. 19.
53. Martial, *Epigrams*, vol. 1, p. 27.
54. Augustus, *Res gestae*, in Naphtali Lewis and Meyer Reinhold, eds., *Roman Civilization: Sourcebook II: The Empire*. New York: Harper and Row, 1966, p. 16.

Chapter 5: The Great Gladiator Rebellion of Spartacus

55. Plutarch, *Life of Crassus*, in *Fall of the Roman Republic*, p. 122.
56. Appian, *Roman History*, excerpted in *Appian: The Civil Wars*, trans. John Carter. New York: Penguin, 1996, p. 65.
57. Plutarch, *Life of Crassus*, in *Fall of the Roman Republic*, p. 122.
58. Appian, *Civil Wars*, p. 65.
59. Plutarch, *Life of Crassus*, in *Fall of the Roman Republic*, p. 122.
60. Appian, *Civil Wars*, p. 65.
61. Frontinus, *Stratagems*, in *The Stratagems and the Aqueducts of Rome*, trans. C.E. Bennett. Cambridge, Mass.: Harvard University Press, 1993, p. 49.
62. Plutarch, *Life of Crassus*, in *Fall of the Roman Republic*, p. 124.
63. Plutarch, *Life of Crassus*, in *Fall of the Roman Republic*, p. 124.

64. Plutarch, *Life of Crassus*, in *Fall of the Roman Republic*, p. 124.
65. Plutarch, *Life of Crassus*, in *Fall of the Roman Republic*, p. 125.
66. Plutarch, *Life of Crassus*, in *Fall of the Roman Republic*, p. 126.
67. Frontinus, *Stratagems*, p. 157.
68. Frontinus, *Stratagems*, p. 158.
69. Plutarch, *Life of Crassus*, in *Fall of the Roman Republic*, p. 127.
70. Appian, *Civil Wars*, p. 67.

Chapter 6: Social and Moral Aspects of Amphitheater Fights

71. Calpurnius Flaccus, *Declamatio*, quoted in Carlin A. Barton, *The Sorrow of the Ancient Romans: The Gladiator and the Monster.* Princeton, N.J.: Princeton University Press, 1993, p. 12.
72. Martial, *Epigrams*, vol. 1, pp. 377–79.
73. Cicero, *Tusculan Disputations*, quoted in Barton, *Sorrow of the Ancient Romans*, p. 18.
74. Seneca, *On Providence*, in Hadas, *Stoic Philosophy of Seneca*, pp. 37–38.
75. Tertullian, *On the Spectacles*, quoted in Barton, *Sorrow of the Ancient Romans*, p. 12.
76. Seneca, *Natural Questions*, quoted in Barton, *Sorrow of the Ancient Romans*, p. 56.
77. Seneca, *Moral Letters*, in Hadas, *Stoic Philosophy of Seneca*, p. 172.
78. Seneca, *Moral Letters*, in Hadas, *Stoic Philosophy of Seneca*, pp. 205–207.
79. Quoted in Shelton, *As the Romans Did*, pp. 346–47.
80. Quoted in Shelton, *As the Romans Did*, p. 347.
81. Pliny the Elder, *Natural History*, p. 111.

Epilogue: The Decline of the Gladiator

82. The only pagan emperor who sat on the throne after Constantine's passing was Julian, who ruled from 361 to 363. Julian attempted to deemphasize Christianity in favor of Rome's pagan traditions, but he met with opposition and also died young, leaving his successors to reverse his policies and support the Christians.
83. Seneca, *Moral Letters*, in Lewis and Reinhold, *Roman Civilization: Sourcebook II*, p. 611.

Glossary

aedile: An official in charge of maintaining public buildings and overseeing public games.

amphitheater: A wooden or stone structure, usually oval shaped and open at the top, in which the ancient Romans staged public games and shows, including gladiatorial fights.

andabate: A gladiator who fought while blindfolded by a helmet with no eyeholes.

bestiarius (**plural,** *bestiarii*): "Beast man"; an arena hunter who may have had a lower status or used a different fighting style than a *venator*.

bustuarii: "Tomb men"; warriors who fought at funerals, constituting early versions of gladiators.

catervarii: "Group fighters"; gladiators who fought in groups rather than pairs.

dictata: Lessons, rules, or orders.

dimachaerius: A gladiator who fought without a shield, using two swords, one in each hand.

doctores: "Teachers"; trainers of gladiators and other arena fighters.

equite: A gladiator who fought on horseback.

essedarius (**plural,** *essedarii*): A gladiator who fought from a moving chariot.

familia gladiatorum: "Family of gladiators"; the group of gladiators under the charge of a *lanista*.

gladiatrix: A woman gladiator.

gladius: The sword wielded by Roman soldiers and several types of gladiators, and the word from which "gladiator" was derived.

hoplomachus: A kind of gladiator, either the same as or very similar to a Samnite.

infamia: "Bad reputation"; a social stigma shared by Roman actors, gladiators, and other public performers.

lanista (**plural,** *lanistae*): A professional supplier of gladiators.

laquearius: A gladiator whose principal weapon was the lasso.

ludus (**plural,** *ludi*): A public game show in ancient Rome; also, the school where arena fighters trained.

Morituri te salutant!: "Those about to die salute you!"; the phrase recited by gladiators just prior to combat.

munerarius: The magistrate in charge of the amphitheater shows.

munus (**plural,** *munera*): "Offering" or "duty"; a public show involving gladiators.

myrmillo (**plural,** *myrmillones*): "Fishman"; a kind of gladiator, similar to a Samnite but less heavily armored.

naumachia (**plural,** *naumachiae*): A staged sea battle.

noxii ad gladium ludi damnati: "Condemned to be killed by the sword in the games"; a death sentence to be carried out in the arena.

obscaenus: Indecent, filthy, or loathsome.

ordinarii: "Ordinary gladiators"; gladiators who fought in pairs.

palus: A six-foot-tall wooden pole used by gladiatorial trainees as a stand-in for an opponent; also refers to a team of gladiators in the school.

panem et circenses: "Bread and circuses"; an informal term for the Roman government policy of distributing free food to the urban masses while heavily subsidizing the public games and shows.

parma: A small round shield used by Thracian warriors and gladiators.

perditus: Hopeless, ruined, or lost.

pompa: The paradelike ceremony that opened gladiatorial fights, chariot races, and other spectacles.

primus palus: The most skilled and feared group of gladiators in a barracks; the *secundus palus* was the second-best, and so on.

probatio armorum: The inspection of gladiators' weapons just prior to combat.

procurator (plural, *procuratores*): The manager of a gladiator school in imperial times.

retiarius (plural, *retiarii*): "Net wielder"; a kind of gladiator who wore no armor and carried a net and a long trident.

rudis: A wooden sword used by training gladiators; the *rudis* was also a symbol of a retiring gladiator.

sagitarii: Arena fighters who used bows and arrows to slaughter animals.

Samnite: A member of a fierce central-Italian hill tribe conquered by the Romans during the early Republic; also, a kind of gladiator attired as a Samnite warrior—heavily armored and carrying a sword and heavy shield.

scutum: The rectangular shield carried by Roman soldiers and also by certain gladiators, including the *myrmillones* and Samnites.

secutor (plural, *secutores*): A kind of gladiator, either the same as or very similar to a Samnite.

sica: A curved short sword wielded by Thracian warriors and gladiators.

sine missione: "To the death"; a kind of gladiatorial combat in which the combatants had to continue fighting until one was killed.

stans missus: The condition of a gladiator who attained a draw.

Thracian: A native of the northern Greek region of Thrace; also a gladiator attired as a Thracian warrior—lightly armored and carrying a curved sword and small round shield.

venatio (plural, *venationes*): "Hunt"; any of various animal shows that took place in an amphitheater.

venator (plural, *venatores*): "Hunter"; an arena performer who fought and killed animals.

For Further Reading

Gladiatorial Fights and Other Entertainment

Robert B. Kebric, *Roman People*. Mountain View, Calif.: Mayfield, 2001. This volume by one of the leading scholars of ancient Rome contains an excellent, very readable chapter about Roman chariot racing.

John Malam, *Secret Worlds: Gladiators*. London: Dorling Kindersley, 2002. A beautifully illustrated book that brings the exciting but bloody gladiatorial combats of ancient Rome to life.

Don Nardo, *Greek and Roman Theater*. San Diego: Lucent Books, 1995. This volume covers the less violent forms of Roman entertainment, including plays, mimes, street theater, and poetry recitations.

———, *Roman Amphitheaters*. New York: Franklin Watts, 2002. Tells about the origins of the stone arenas where gladiators and animal hunters fought and often died, how these structures were built, and the variety of games they showcased.

Richard Watkins, *Gladiator*. Boston: Houghton Mifflin, 1997. A very well written, nicely illustrated overview of gladiators and their world for young readers.

Roman Daily Life

Lionel Casson, *Daily Life in Ancient Rome*. New York: American Heritage, 1975. A well-written presentation of how the Romans lived: their homes, streets, entertainment, foods, theaters, religion, slaves, marriage customs, and more.

Anthony Marks and Graham Tingay, *The Romans*. London: Usborne, 1990. An excellent summary of the main aspects of Roman history, life, and arts, supported by hundreds of beautiful and accurate drawings reconstructing Roman times. Aimed at basic readers but highly recommended for anyone interested in Roman civilization.

Jonathan Rutland, *See Inside a Roman Town*. New York: Barnes and Noble, 1986. A very attractively illustrated introduction to some major concepts of Roman civilization for basic readers.

Judith Simpson, *Ancient Rome*. New York: Time-Life, 1997. One of the best entries in Time-Life's library of picture books about the ancient world, this one is beautifully illustrated with attractive and appropriate photographs and paintings. The general but well-written text is aimed at intermediate young readers.

Roman History and Warfare

Isaac Asimov, *The Roman Empire*. Boston: Houghton Mifflin, 1967. An excellent overview of the main events of the Empire; so precise and clearly written that even very basic readers will benefit.

Peter Connolly, *Greece and Rome at War*. London: Macdonald, 1981. A highly informative and useful volume by one of the finest historians of ancient military affairs. Highly recommended for advanced or ambitious young readers or even just for the many stunning color illustrations (by Connolly himself).

Don Nardo, *The Ancient Romans*. San Diego: Lucent Books, 2001. Discusses Rome's origins, how it conquered Italy and then the rest of the Mediterranean world, how it prospered for many centuries, and finally how it succumbed to the so-called barbarian invasions in the fifth century.

Chester G. Starr, *The Ancient Romans.* New York: Oxford University Press, 1971. A clearly written survey of Roman history, featuring several interesting sidebars on such subjects as the Etruscans, Roman law, and the Roman army. Also contains many primary-source quotes by Roman and Greek writers. For intermediate and advanced younger readers.

Major Works Consulted

Ancient Sources in Translation

Appian, *Appian: The Civil Wars.* Trans. John Carter. New York: Penguin, 1996.

Frontinus, *The Stratagems and the Aqueducts of Rome.* Trans. C.E. Bennett. Cambridge, Mass.: Harvard University Press, 1993.

Homer, *Iliad.* Trans. W.H.D. Rouse. New York: New American Library, 1950.

Juvenal, *Satires,* published as *Juvenal: The Sixteen Satires.* Trans. Peter Green. New York: Penguin, 1974.

Livy, *The History of Rome from Its Foundation.* Books 1–5 published as *Livy: The Early History of Rome.* Trans. Aubrey de Sélincourt. New York: Penguin, 1960; books 21–30 published as *Livy: The War with Hannibal.* Trans. Aubrey de Sélincourt. New York: Penguin, 1972; books 31–45 published as *Livy: Rome and the Mediterranean.* Trans. Henry Bettenson. New York: Penguin, 1976. Also, various books excerpted in *Livy.* Vol. 2. Trans. Canon Roberts. New York: E.P. Dutton, 1912.

Martial, *Epigrams.* Ed. and Trans. D.R. Shackleton Bailey. 3 vols. Cambridge, Mass.: Harvard University Press, 1993.

Naphtali Lewis and Meyer Reinhold, eds., *Roman Civilization: Sourcebook II: The Empire.* New York: Harper and Row, 1966. Contains several English translations of original documents relating to Roman entertainment.

Petronius, *The Satyricon.* Trans. J.P. Sullivan. New York: Penguin, 1977.

Pliny the Elder, *Pliny the Elder: Natural History: A Selection.* Trans. John H. Healy. New York: Penguin, 1991.

Plutarch, *Fall of the Roman Republic: Six Lives by Plutarch.* Trans. Rex Warner. New York: Penguin, 1972. Contains the lives of Marius, Sulla, Crassus, Pompey, Caesar, and Cicero; and *Makers of Rome: Nine Lives by Plutarch.* Trans. Ian Scott-Kilvert. New York: Penguin, 1988. Contains the lives of Coriolanus, Fabius Maximus, Marcellus, Cato the Elder, Tiberius Gracchus, Gaius Gracchus, Sertorius, Brutus, and Mark Antony.

Seneca, *Moral Letters.* Trans. Richard M. Gummere. London: William Heinemann, 1918; and assorted works in Moses Hadas, trans. and ed., *The Stoic Philosophy of Seneca.* New York: W.W. Norton, 1958.

Jo-Ann Shelton, ed., *As the Romans Did: A Sourcebook in Roman Social History.* New York: Oxford University Press, 1988. Contains English translations of numerous ancient documents pertaining to Roman leisure activities, including the games and spectacles.

Suetonius, *Lives of the Twelve Caesars,* published as *The Twelve Caesars.* Trans. Robert Graves. Rev. Michael Grant. New York: Penguin, 1979.

Tacitus, *The Annals,* published as *The Annals of Ancient Rome.* Trans. Michael Grant. New York: Penguin, 1989.

Terence, complete surviving works in *Terence: The Comedies.* Trans. Betty Radice. New York: Penguin, 1976.

Vitruvius, *On Architecture.* Trans. Frank Granger. 2 vols. Cambridge, Mass.: Harvard University Press, 1962.

Modern Sources

Roland Auguet, *Cruelty and Civilization: The Roman Games.* London: Routledge, 1994. A commendable overview of Roman games, including gladiatorial combats, *naumachiae* (staged sea battles), wild beast hunts, chariot races, circus factions, and the layout of circuses and amphitheaters.

Alan Baker, *The Gladiator: The Secret History of Rome's Warrior Slaves.* New York: St. Martin's Press, 2000. An excellent general discussion of Roman gladiators, including the political and social dimensions of their combats as well as the kinds of fighters and how they fought. Highly recommended.

J.P.V.D. Balsdon, *Life and Leisure in Ancient Rome.* New York: McGraw-Hill, 1969. This huge, detailed, and masterful volume by a highly respected historian is one of the best general studies of Roman life, customs, and traditions. In addition to sections on exercise, festivals, arena games, wild animal shows, chariot races, and Greek sports (as practiced by the Romans), it contains fulsome discussions of Roman theater, mimes and pantomimes, children's games, family life, schooling, slavery, dining habits, public baths, and more.

Richard C. Beacham, *Spectacle Entertainments of Early Imperial Rome.* New Haven, Conn.: Yale University Press, 1999. This fine study of the famous Roman games is highlighted by first-class scholarship and an excellent bibliography.

Jean-Claude Golvin, *Amphitheaters and Gladiators.* Paris: CNRS Presses, 1990. The definitive modern work on ancient Roman amphitheaters, the structures built to house gladiatorial combats. Highly recommended for serious students of the subject.

Michael Grant, *Gladiators.* New York: Delacorte Press, 1967. One of the most prolific modern classical historians delivers a highly comprehensive and readable general study of the subject.

Eckart Kohne, ed., *Gladiators and Caesars: The Power of Spectacle in Ancient Rome.* Berkeley and Los Angeles: University of California Press, 2000. An in-depth, insightful, very well written treatment of the subject. Highly recommended.

Stephen Wisdom, *Gladiators: 100 B.C.–A.D. 200.* Oxford, England: Osprey, 2001. An extremely well illustrated presentation of the basic facts about Roman gladiators, with numerous photos of amphitheaters and relevant artifacts and several stunning color reconstructions by noted artist Angus McBride. However, nonscholars need to beware that the text of this volume contains a considerable number of factual errors; therefore, they should approach it with caution.

Additional Works Consulted

Books

Lesley Adkins and Roy A. Adkins, *Handbook to Life in Ancient Rome.* New York: Facts On File, 1994.

Carlin A. Barton, *The Sorrow of the Ancient Romans: The Gladiator and the Monster.* Princeton, N.J.: Princeton University Press, 1993.

J.B. Bury, *History of the Later Roman Empire.* 2 vols. 1923. Reprint, New York: Dover, 1958.

Alan Cameron, *Circus Factions: Blues and Greens at Rome and Byzantium.* London: Clarendon Press, 1976.

Tim Cornell and John Matthews, *Atlas of the Roman World.* New York: Facts On File, 1982.

F.R. Cowell, *Life in Ancient Rome.* New York: G.P. Putnam's Sons, 1961.

Alison Futrell, *Blood in the Arena: The Spectacle of Roman Power.* Austin: University of Texas Press, 1998.

Michael Grant, *The World of Rome.* New York: New American Library, 1960.

Harold Johnston, *The Private Life of the Romans.* New York: Cooper Square, 1973.

Senatore R. Lanciani, *Ancient and Modern Rome.* New York: Cooper Square, 1963.

Vera Olivova, *Sport and Games in the Ancient World.* New York: St. Martin's Press, 1984.

Michael B. Poliakoff, *Combat Sports in the Ancient World.* New Haven, Conn.: Yale University Press, 1987.

Peter Quennell, *The Colosseum.* New York: Newsweek Book Division, 1971.

Jon Solomon, *The Ancient World in the Cinema.* New Haven, Conn.: Yale University Press, 2001.

Thomas E.J. Wiedemann, *Emperors and Gladiators.* London: Routledge, 1992.

L.P. Wilkinson, *The Roman Experience.* Lanham, Md.: University Press of America, 1974.

David C. Young, *The Olympic Myth of Greek Amateur Athletics.* Chicago: Ares, 1984.

Internet Sources

Graham Ashford, "The Classic Stance," *Ludus Gladiatorius,* 2002. www.ludus.org.uk.

———, "Dimachaerius," *Ludus Gladiatorius,* 2002. www.ludus.org.uk.

———, "Women Gladiators," *Ludus Gladiatorius,* 2002. www.ludus.org.uk.

Howard Fast, "Spartacus: An Interview with Howard Fast," *AncientSites,* June 28, 2000. www.trussel.com.

Kathleen Coleman, "The Virtues of Violence: Gladiators, the Arena, and the Roman System of Values," (lecture delivered at the College of the Holy Cross, Worcester, Mass., March 2001). www.psg.com/~ted/vaninst/VbColeman.html.

Periodicals

Allen Ward, "The Movie *Gladiator* in Historical Perspective," *New England Classical News Letter,* May 2001.

Index

Achilles, 16
Achillia, 49
Aeneas, 16
"Age of Heroes," 81
Agrippina, 27
Ajax, 16
Amazons, 49
Apennine Mountains, 18
Appian, 66
Apulia, Italy, 72
Ashford, Graham
  on classic gladiator
    stance, 35–36
  on evidence of female
    gladiators, 50
  on tactics of
    dimachaerius gladiator,
    45
Auguet, Roland
  description of gladiators'
    barracks at Pompeii,
    33
Augustus (emperor of
  Rome), 24

Baker, Alan
  on general description
    of spectators and
    fighters, 22
  on gladiators and
    Roman hypocrisy,
    29–30
Batiatus, Lentulus, 66,
  69–70

Brutus Pera, Decimus,
  20
Brutus Pera, Marcus, 20

Caesar, Julius, 25, 72
  establishment of
    gladiator school by,
    24
  monopoly on
    procurement and
    training of gladiators
    by, 30
  use of contests for
    popularity by, 23–24
Caligula, 44
  sparring match and, 42
Cameron, Alan
  on use of games to
    divert public
    concerns, 27
Campania, Italy, 17, 20,
  66
Campus Martius, 64
Cannicus, 74–75
Capua, 66, 69
Carophorus, 63
Carrhae (Mesopotamia),
  72
Carthage, 20
Castus, 74
Celts, 45
Christians
  political triumph of,
    89–90

view of gladiators by,
  11, 82
Cicero
  concern for animals by,
    86
  dislike of contests by,
    85–86
  on submission to
    authority, 80
Cisalpine Gaul, 73
Civil Wars, The (Appian),
  66
Claudius (emperor of
  Rome), 61
Clodianus, C. Lentulus
  defeat of, 73
Coleman, Kathleen, 37,
  39
  on object of training, 25
Colosseum, 33
  animal hunts in, 91
  execution of Christians
    in, 90
  use of for public
    executions, 63
Constantine (emperor of
  Rome), 90
Constantinople, 89
Crassus, Marcus Licinius,
  72, 77
Crixus, 71, 72
crucifixion, 77

Davies, Delmer, 44

use of, as propaganda,
40, 53
Pollice Verso (painting),
60
Pompeii, Italy, 10, 17
banning of gladiatorial
contests in, 53
description of gladiator
school at, 32
first stone
amphitheater
established in,
18–19
gladiators' barracks at,
33
graffiti found at, 10, 28
Pompey, 72–73, 85–86
Porcius, 19
Publicola, L. Gellius, 72

Rhegium, Italy, 73
Romans
acceptance of capital
punishment by, 84
cultural love of violence
and, 10, 12, 23
differing views on
gladiators by, 10–11
Greek culture and,
15–16
hypocrisy of, 29
notions of honor and
submission to
authority and, 80
superiority of, 13
value system of, 12–14
wars against the
Samnites and, 18, 20

Rome
decline of, 91–92
fear of Spartacus in,
71–72
first known gladiatorial
contest in, 20
last slave rebellion in,
77

Salamis, 64
Samnites, 18
equipment of, 22
invasion of Campania
by, 20
as original gladiator
type, 40
relationship between
Roman soldier and, 41
Sarsina, Italy, 79
Second Punic War, 20
Senate
debarring Pompeii from
holding contests by,
53
political concerns of,
about contests, 24
Seneca the Younger
on dislike for some
aspects of contests,
33, 84–85
on gladiators' oath, 31
on harmful moral
effects of contests,
11
Severus, Septimius, 50
Silarus River, 76
Spartacus, 18, 24
background of, 68

building of slave army
by, 71
early victories of, 70
escape of, 69–70
final battle of, 75–77
freeing of slaves by, 66
pirates and, 73
Spartacus (Fast), 66, 67
Spartacus (film), 14
depiction of gladiator
school in, 38
photograph from, 30
Storax, C. Lucius, 78
Suetonius, 44
on Ceasar's use of
gladiatorial contests,
24
Sulla, 72

Terence, 23
Tertullian, 11
concerns about
gladiatorial contests
and, 82
denunciation of
contests by, 90
on murder in the
amphitheater, 11
Theodoric the Ostrogoth,
91
Theodosius I (emperor of
Rome), 90
Thrace, 68, 69
Tiber River, 20
Tiberius (emperor of
Rome), 48
Titus (emperor of Rome),
64

Picture Credits

Cover Photo: ©Bettmann/CORBIS
©PIZZOLI ALBERTO/CORBIS SYGMA, 34, 35, 36, 78
©Archivo Iconografico, S.A./CORBIS, 22, 29
The Art Archive/Museo della Civilta Romana Rome/Dagli Orti, 87
Associated Press/SEG SPORTS INC., 13
©Bettmann/CORBIS, 19, 31, 38, 40, 55, 56, 60, 79
Blackbirch, 91
Bridgeman Art Library, 58, 72
©ARNOLD CEDRIC/CORBIS SYGMA, 50

Dover Publications, 17, 21, 65
©Mimmo Jodice/CORBIS, 18
Joseph Paris Picture Archive, 23, 84, 89
©The Kobal Collection, 11, 30, 43, 44, 48, 61, 62, 67, 68, 70, 76
Mary Evans Picture Library, 37, 49, 75, 81, 83
North Wind Picture Archives, 16, 26, 51, 52
©Stapleton Collection/CORBIS, 46
©Gian Berto Vanni/CORBIS, 32
©Roger Wood/CORBIS, 41
Steve Zmina, 69, 71, 74

About the Author

Historian Don Nardo has published many volumes about ancient Roman history and culture, including *The Punic Wars, The Age of Augustus, A Travel Guide to Ancient Rome, Life of a Roman Slave, The Greenhaven Encyclopedia of Greek and Roman Mythology,* and biographies of Julius Caesar and Cleopatra. Mr. Nardo also writes screenplays and teleplays and composes music. He lives in Massachusetts with his wife, Christine.